under the quandong tree

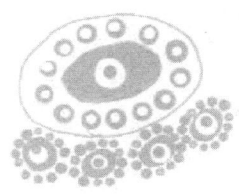

under the quandong tree
Minmia

Quandong Dreaming Publishing

First published in Australia in 2007 by
Quandong Dreaming Publishing
5 Park Street
Mogo NSW 2536

©Maureen Smith 2007
Reprinted 2009.

All rights reserved.

This book is copyright. Except as permitted under the Copyright Act 1968 (for example a fair dealing for the purposes of study, research, criticism or review) no part of this book may be reproduced, stored in a retrieval system, or transmitted in any form or by any means without prior permission of the author/publisher.

Cataloguing-in-Publication Data
National Library of Australia

Minmia (Maureen Smith), 1947–
Under the quandong tree

ISBN 978 0 646 48348 1 (pbk.)

Creation—Mythology.
Dreamtime (Aboriginal Australian mythology).
Wiradjuri (Australian people)—Folklore.
Wiradjuri (Australian people)—Religion.
Women, Aboriginal Australian—Folklore.
Women, Aboriginal Australian—Religion.
Aboriginal Australians—Folklore.
Aboriginal Australians—Religion.

299.9215

Book and cover design by
Vicki Russell

Original artwork by
Maureen Smith

Cover artwork by
Gilion Phillips

Cover photograph by
Irene Lorbergs

Printed in Australia by
Ligare Pty Ltd
138 Bonds Road Riverwood NSW 2210

The paper used to produce this book was manufactured in Australia from pulp sourced from sustainable forests.

The cover photograph is of Minmia and her grand-daughter Makenzie Smith.

My loving thanks to all of you wonderful migai (women) who endured the task of ensuring that this work was made fit for all to read, which being women's business made for a difficult time.

Michal and Jillian, I'm sure you have both earned your wings. This task has had every conceivable obstacle thrown at us to prevent this journey going to paper. My wish for all who read this is if it brings change to your life that is for the better, just send a blessing to those who worked so hard for it.

Gundrah ah,
Minmia

CONTENTS

Introduction xiii
Preface xv

Part One

Chapter 1   The Teachings................................. 3
Chapter 2   Creation...................................... 10
            • The Story of How the Bunyip Came to Be 14
Chapter 3   Dreaming 17
            • The Oneness 18
            • The Story of the Giant Green Ant
              and the Golden Sunset Spider................. 21
            • Dreaming Tracks 25
            • The Story of Burradahn, Son of Biami 35
Chapter 4   Songlines 42
            • Born on the Songlines 43
            • Songlines for Nienoj 45
              – Bandicoot 46
              – She-oak 47
              – Honey Grevillea 48
              – Turtle 49
              – Wombat 50
            • Songlines for Esme 51
              – Tribal 51
              – Koala 53
              – Brolga 53
            • Songlines for Kara 55
              – Kangaroo 55

	– Magpie	56
	– Hawk	58
	• The Essence of that Contained	58
	• Singing Up	61
	• Finding your Songlines	62
Chapter 5	Miwi	66
	• Awakening Your Miwi	67
	• The Miwi Print	71
	• Rebirthing	75
	• Rebirthing Ceremony	75
	• The Miwi	77
	• Miwi Energy	79
	• Divining Miwi Energy	81
	• What Connects the Miwi to the Journey	83
	• Exercising Your Senses	84
	• Intimacy	84
	• What Disconnects the Miwi from Its Journey	87
	• What Keeps the Miwi Connected	90
	• Miwi Connectedness Maintenance	91
	• Cleansing a Child's Miwi	92

Part Two

Chapter 6	The Journey — The Birthing Ceremony	96
	• Plant Essences	97
	• The Ceremony	99
	• How to Conduct a Birthing Ceremony	100

Chapter 7	The Journey — Age and Responsibilities	104
	• The Story of Dinawahn	107
	• The Five Life Stages	109
	– Boodthoong: from birth to three years old	110
	– Boori: from three to between twelve and fifteen years old	111
	– Wanai: from twelve to fifteen years old to between twenty-seven and thirty years old	113
	– Migai or Yinarr: from thirty to fifty years old	115
	– Memee: once you're a grandmother, or from fifty years old until you die	115
Chapter 8	The Journey — Intimacy with our Opponents	117
	• How to Become Intimate	124
	• Teaching Story on Love — How the Waratah Became Red	127
	• Getting to Know Love	129
	• Teaching Story on Acceptance and Unconditional Love — How the Platypus Came to Be	133
	• Getting to Know Tolerance	136
	• Getting to Know Acceptance and Patience	137
	• Teaching Story on Fear — How Courage Was Born	138
	• Getting to Know Fear and Courage	140
	• Teaching Story on Greed — The Brolgas and the Pelicans	143
	• Getting to Know Greed	144
	• Getting to Know Ego	146
	• Getting to Know Vanity	147
	• Teaching Story on Compassion — How the Kangaroo Got Her Pouch	148

Part Three

Chapter 9 The Story of the Eight Sisters 152

- The Killing of the Seven Sisters 153
- The Escape of the Eighth Sister 154
- The Collapse of the Eighth Sister 154
- The Wirrinun's Attempt to Duplicate the Power Stone 155
- Wuuluumbin (Mount Warning) Today 156

Chapter 10 The Breaking of Biami's Stones 158

- Biami's Stones 159
- The Decision to Bring Back the Lore/Law and to Break Biami's Stones 160
- The Breaking and the Opening of the Dreaming Tracks 162
- The Stones for Re-joining and Strengthening the Dreaming Tracks 164
- An Earth Walk 167
- Moving to the New Dreaming Track 174
- Closing the Dreaming Tracks 176
- The New Dreaming Track. 178
- What We can Do to Stabilise 180

Endnotes. 184

Glossary 186

List of Illustrations

Illustration 1 – The Miwi

Illustration 2 – The First Born

Illustration 3 – A Dreaming Track

Illustration 4 – Songlines Map 1

Illustration 5 – Songlines Map 2

Illustration 6 – Songlines Map 3

Illustration 7 – A Child's Dreaming Story

Illustration 8 – Miwi with Feelers and Eyes

Illustration 9 – Miwi with Dahwie and Mullahwahl

Illustration 10 – Miwi with Pollution

Illustration 11 – Sacred Water Spring Location

Illustration 12 – The Journey and Our Opponents

INTRODUCTION

Minmia is an Aboriginal senior woman, educator and healer. She is a custodian of traditional women's lore/law of the Wirradjirri people, an Aboriginal nation in New South Wales stretching from Dunedoo into Victoria.

In 1987 the decision was made by some people of the lore/law in Australia to no longer keep the teachings secret. Mother Earth was suffering from the massive scale of humanity's destructiveness and Indigenous Australia responded.

Minmia was instructed to pass down Wirradjirri women's lore/law to any women interested. For many years she taught at women's camps and gatherings where Indigenous elders, ordained women of different faiths, Indigenous women and non-Indigenous women attended. Minmia was often encouraged to put her oral teachings in a written form and so, to facilitate this, from 1998 to 2002 recordings were made of some of her teaching weekends.

The location of the weekends moved over the years. Minmia taught on her own land when she lived on a farm at Wauchope, New South Wales. After meeting Sister Angela, an Anglican Clare nun, at a conference on 'Women and Spirituality' at Wuuluumbin (Mount Warning) in the early 1990s, Minmia was invited to hold her teaching weekends at the 'Community of Saint Clare' at Stroud. These weekends continued until 1998 when Minmia returned to full-time work.

Ill health laid Minmia low for about two years and then further teaching weekends were organised in Sydney, firstly at St Xavier's Church Hall, Lavender Bay, North Sydney and then at the NSW Writers' Centre, Callan Park, Rozelle. The teachings given at the Sydney weekends were recorded with Minmia's permission. Minmia then decided that the weekends were not as effective as they could be because they were not residential so the weekends were moved to Vijayaloka, the retreat centre for the Friends of the Western Buddhist Order at Campbelltown, New South Wales.

The last three of the recorded teaching weekends were called

'Women's Business — Minmia's Sit Down and Grow up Weekends'. This title was used because of the visit of the Tall Ones after the workshop held ten days after 11 September 2001. We, the organisers, had worked very hard, we thought, but the Tall Ones told Minmia that no-one had done any work and we were no longer to call the weekends 'workshops' but 'Sit Down and Grow Up Weekends'.

Many women attended and assisted with the weekends. Several helped with the organisation and taping of the talks and a number continued to be involved in this book project for some years, transcribing the tapes and helping with the collating and editing process. Two of us continued to work closely with Minmia for a further three to four years and helped bring this book to its publication.

Michal Armstrong
Bronte, Sydney
October 2007

PREFACE

My name is Minmia, which is 'the messenger of birds'. If I want to contact anybody or say hello you'll find yourself being stalked by magpies. Don't be afraid because that's my totem.

I am a Wirradjirri woman. Wirradjirri country runs from Dunedoo in New South Wales right down into Victoria, and from the Blue Mountains to Lake Cargelligo bordering onto Parkingee country. It's country for the biggest tribe in New South Wales. This is the riverland of the Murrumbidgee, Killara (Lachlan) and Macquarie rivers.

I want to take you on a walk with me, a walk I hope will change the way you see the world and your place in it. My wish is that, in the difficult times in which we live, reading this book will give you a greater understanding of yourself and tolerance of others.

I'm Murdoo's great-grand-daughter and I was born down a line of women to carry Wirradjirri women's lore/law. My great-great-grandmother comes from the Gurindji line and my great-great-grandfather from Pitjantjatjara so I have connections there. I've been one of the very fortunate people who have been able to learn some of the lore/law.

Some years ago now, one of my old aunties, my great-aunty, was caught doing a ceremony and taken to a mental institution and locked up there for thirty-eight years, where she died. So, the fear of not offending the Christian God has had dreadful consequences for my people. For a long time our teachings went underground and some were lost entirely, breaking the teaching lines. I wasn't allowed to teach any of this until 1990. For many Indigenous communities this was the time the old people called back the lore/law because so many bad things were happening. This was done through ceremony; one of these ceremonies was the breaking of the sacred stones Biami left behind for the purpose of restoring what is right.1

I was born to a Koori mother and a white father. This antagonised some of my old aunties when they were told I would carry the Wirrloo line. But the tradition is the line is carried through the women; even my cousin Ivan inherited his lore/law line through the same great-grandmother.

Our teachings became almost extinct under a tsunami of Christianity. Many of the remaining stories, songs and teachings were passed on through the paddocks when Kooris were doing all the seasonal fruit picking etc. In many cases this was where the Aboriginal Protection Board and Christian 'thought police' never bothered to go. Too hot or too wet and too many flies and kids with snotty noses, I guess. However, it served its purpose in keeping and passing on what little lore/law remained. This is why some of the words I use are not Wirradjirri, but I have tried to maintain the integrity of what I heard many years ago.

I was taught in secret, from the time I was about six years old by my great-grandmother. I was thirteen, just a wanai, when she died. And I was nineteen when Subbina died. Subbina was a wirrloo (powerful healer/teacher) and she was older than the Lachlan River. She had been here many times and Subbina is still around me. Since Subbina I have had many teachers — not only from many places in my country, but also from around the world. I am also guided and rescued by the Tall Ones; these are great beings that have never been born.

One of the most profound teachings that I have ever received was from a five-year-old girl called Amy Edwards. I was invited to Amy's friend's birthday party to meet her very best friend. I don't remember the friend's name but I remember Amy. She was everything one would expect of a beautiful 'Australian' child — cute, blonde, blue-eyed. We arrived at the party and she took me through the house to the backyard where all the children were playing. I asked her which one was her best friend. Amy replied, 'The little girl in the corner in the pink dress.'

The little girl in the corner in the pink dress who Amy had pointed to was the only child at the party who was black, really black. I realised that the true Amy was far deeper than the blonde hair and blue eyes. This was one of the most sacred teachings I have ever received. It made me look beyond and spread my awareness much deeper. Teachings come in many shapes and forms, and often by way of unexpected opportunities, so don't let them pass you by.

As I have said, I was born into the Wirradjiri nation to take up part of the Wirradjiri women's lore/law. How much do I know? I'll tell you how much I know. Let's say all the teachings in this country amount to one handful of sand. The teachings I know would amount to one grain. So you know, I'm not wise. I might look wise, I have grey hair and I've earned every one of them. But I'm not 'walking wisdom'. I teach the teachings that were given to me. I struggle every day, like every single person does, with my conscience, with my way of life, with right and wrong, with ego, all of those things that weaken my Miwi. I struggle just like you do. So revere the wisdom from the teachings and just leave me as the tongue or the voice or the noise it makes.

Minmia

Part One

Chapter 1

THE TEACHINGS

The quandong tree is sacred to Wirradjirri country. It was a major food source and was sought after for its tart sweetness. Much of the lore/law, teachings and teaching stories were passed down while processing the fruits of the quandong tree. The fruit itself was taken and prepared for drying, and the nuts gathered for the making of adornments.

When I was a child, a lot of time was spent under the quandong trees that grew prolifically in my country. The name of this book comes from the memories I have of hearing the stories told to me under the quandong tree. I think we would all live in a happier world if every old woman took a young woman and sat with her under a tree and shared her story.

Let's now talk about the teachings. The lore/law says that we are born 'boss of self'. We walk our journey boss of self. So take your power, walk your talk, seek your truth and be your journey and hopefully when you die, you die boss of self.

There are the men's teachings, women's teachings, and our teachings. The teachings are passed down in stories and stones. The men's teaching stones are called Tjuringa; the women's stones, Ogkteringa. Both men and women have sacred teaching stones. These stones are carved with symbols that represent a teaching/ceremony. My great-granny's stones were very old and worn; she used them to get answers and prophecies for people as well as in ceremony. I'm sure she had over fifty stones. Muulbung, the old kadaitchi (lore/law man) also had his stones. He would say to my great-granny, 'I will talk with these' and you would hear them as he moved his bag. Each one of these stones is a teaching. For example, about how greed was born, or how courage was born, and every stone had answers. The stones I paint today are different to the originals because I am fearful that people with malice in their hearts might use the real ones to cause untold damage and suffering to others.

So, there is women's business, and then there is men's business. I don't get involved in men's business. It's against the lore/law. Men are the keepers of history, they were the hunters and they were the protectors. There are a lot of men who are looking for this teaching. I can't teach them because I teach women. Because men are often involved in the birth of their children these days, a lot of the old women now say that they're fine to join in. But I still find that really difficult because it was always a matter of women's business, men's business, then our business. I honour men in their masculinity, their maleness, as I honour the female. However, as I don't think I have overstepped the lore/law of women's secret business, this book can be read by men.

Women's business has to do with a way of life that keeps families and communities together supporting each other. It's walking every day and living every day a spirituality of helping each other and especially caring for the Earth, our mother, Nungeena-tya, who is dying around us.

Women are the keepers of the bloodlines and the community developers. They are the nurturers of the environment, of the family, of the family structure, of the kinship lines. They are responsible for the birthing ceremonies and giving honour back to this land, our mother, Nungeena-tya, for what she has given to us. It's very much about taking responsibility for all the children. You see, traditionally children aren't owned by anybody. They belong to everybody. My concern is everywhere I look we have what we now call 'feral children' running wild, Koori and non-Koori alike. We need to take a step back and look at what's gone wrong.

•••••

You can't be at peace with the world until you are at peace with yourself. You can't heal or help heal the world if you are not healing yourself. So part of women's business is women coming together to work on the healing of themselves with support in many ways. Women's business is learning to never judge oneself or another so that the support becomes unconditional. Women look at a whole range of issues that concern women and children, including initiations. Women choose a path that is very close to them, that they have skills for and that they will work on. It's about the traditional way of parenting. Women's business includes medicines, foods, learning about women's sacred places, fertility areas and birthing areas. What is a birthing cave? Why is it there? What is the importance of sacred water? Why and how it should be cared for? What does it mean to us, and how is it important to our very survival?

Women involved in women's business also learn how to traditionally cleanse areas of pain, trauma, bad spirit — to put it in one word, the bugeenge — and how to flush it out. This will allow the protection and safety of our Miwis (spirits, consciousness and souls) on their journeys. It's about bringing back the feminine, the feminine balance of healing, of nurturing — so very, very strong in women — and sending that down to our children. Women need to know where there are sitting places, healing places and thinking places. It's about sharing the song, sharing the dance and sharing the future.

The teachings are important. Why are they important? They are the essence of the fabric of creation and they shouldn't die. The good thing is that you know that you are a seeker of the teachings; that's the good thing. So you aren't just sitting down wrapped up in spider webs. You are actually out there living the search. If the women's teachings die there's a certain essence of women that will die. We have to have something that's sacred to come back to.

If we don't live the journey, that we have been born to live, then we become spiritually lost. So we choose our lives and we choose our teachings. It's important that we know and keep the women's sacred teachings. That's who we are — we're women, and who better to understand and nurture women than ourselves? And the greatest woman of all, the most powerful woman who we need desperately is Nungeena-tya. Our mother the Earth is being raped and pillaged and bludgeoned. She's dying and we really have to look at doing something. If you are a baby feeding at the breast of your mother and your mother dies and there's no other breast then you, the baby, die. And we've got very, very little time.

It's really important to learn about the birthing and the spiritual

Illustration 1. This is the Miwi, universal spirit, attending a Birthing Ceremony. When a child begins its journey it is already connected to spirit; the ceremony is to connect the Miwi's journey print to Nungeena-tya.

attachment to the land. I've been concerned for years for my fellow countrymen. How can they belong to a country that they don't know anything about? They learn about all sorts of other countries, all sorts of nations, other cultures, other traditions, even other religions but they don't know anything about their own heritage. What's really important for all Australians to know is that, believe it or not, if you are born of this land, you are of this land, you have a responsibility to this land and you have a right to know; colour never has had anything to do with it. Why learn about other cultures before you learn about your own spiritual heritage, history and traditions of 60 000 years?

Now it's my job — and not only my job but also other women's jobs — to bring back the stories and tell the teachings: about how vanity was born, how ego was born, all of these things. About why vanity and ego are opponents of ours and how we can learn to walk with them, how we can be intimate with them. A lot of the old teachers have died now and have taken the teachings with them so we need to get the teachings out to all women.

Often a picture speaks a thousand words so look at Illustration 1. This is your Miwi, better known as your spirit, consciousness or soul. If I cut you open with a tin opener and looked inside to the Miwi within, that's what I'd see and that's what is on the journey. Some call it spirit, some call it consciousness, some call it soul, and some call it essence. The body is only to assist the Miwi to physically fulfill its learning tasks. The Miwi has no mouth because our mouths get us into trouble. It's a clear teaching to walk our talk.

I invite you to walk with me in these teachings. At the end of our walk, feel free to say, 'Well, this doesn't apply to me.' However, I ask you to honour your understanding and knowledge of Indigenous peoples' connection to country, to our mother, Nungeena-tya.

I give no guarantee that these teachings are the only teachings, because they are not — far, far from it! I can't even say that the teachings that I have and am handing over to you are not contaminated in some way or to some degree. They have been passed down orally and along the way they have been distorted by pride, ego and so on. All the forces against us brought by colonisation broke the teaching lines. Massacres, stealing the children of kadaitchi (clever men) and wirrloo, new sicknesses, division of the tribes, demonising the teachings, ego, greed and fear took over the lore/law keepers. Fear ruled; it was the greatest killer of the lore/law as many believed the oppressors' god was more powerful than Biami although some have now come full circle to realise they are one and the same.

Before colonisation there were about 700 nations around this country, for example Wirradjirri, Eora, Gurinji, Parkingee, Kimillaroi and Gnunnawahl. And the fact that we were all black didn't mean we were homogenous at all. We had different dreaming stories and different teachings. I am responsible for some of the stories, which means I'm responsible for keeping certain spiritual beliefs alive. It is my job to spiritually take care and talk about them, teach them and honour them.

Other people have other stories to safeguard. We're talking about every single lump, bump, movement, plant, animal and whatever on this planet. Every songline, every dreaming track, you had to know it — and one person can't know it all. I've been at it for years and years and years and years and still I know just a grain of sand. I now feel privileged to have been given a very small part of it for safekeeping. When I was a wanai I wanted no part of the teaching. I just wanted the Hollywood fairy story — marry the man, live in the mansion, have the perfect children, and be the envy of the neighbours. Then one day I looked into the paper bag of my dreams and found it empty. I realised the fairy story was in my mind. The mind is not on the journey, the Miwi is.

I honour all the world's spiritual teachings that have the essence, the purity of truth. However, I also know most of the teachings have been contaminated by us, some accidentally in the process of re-interpretation to another language, and some just to use as a fear-control mechanism. That's all I want to say. I just want to speak my truth as I know it and encourage you to remember always that we, who pass on the teachings, are human with human frailties.

I can say this now with absolute certainty. I have had a blessed life — not just a little bit blessed, an extremely blessed life. Family is very important to me. All families are very important to me — the whole family, not just the children who, of course, are priority, but the whole family, because today the entire family is suffering.

I want to bring back 'thinking' places. I want to bring back the songs. I want to bring back the stories. I want to bring back the sense of belonging. I want to help with the healing. That's what I want.

Chapter 2

CREATION

Let's start with the teachings about Creation, because it's very, very important to understand the lore/law in terms of where we come from and what we give back. There is but one Earth. There is but one humanity. There is but one Creation, and it's very important to be connected to the Oneness. The teachings say — and I believe it with all my heart and spirit — that Creation happened here, in Australia.

A long time ago in the Dreaming, before the first War of the Dreaming, Biami sat and began Creation. Everything was created by Biami. He carried the seeds within Himself from another place. Biami was always in the Dreaming. We are taught that Biami started the Dreamtime. He's made of all the Dreaming tracks, all the Dreamings, all the Rivers of the Dreaming, all the islands in the Rivers of the Dreaming. He is the very essence of the Oneness. You could lie on your back on a clear night and look into the Rivers of the Dreaming and everything you see out there is Biami. If you imagine zillions of eyes looking that much further beyond what you see, that is all Biami, the Creator, all of His essence. It could give you a little indication of what the Oneness means. That is why we are born many, many, many times and we still don't understand it because it is so amazing.

There are very few Miwis who, after living many lives, have reached that level of Oneness and those few that have are the known prophets of many of the teachings. Is it bad to follow these prophets? No, because they too carry this essence of Oneness — the Creator. Allah, Jehovah, Brahma, God, Great Spirit, these are all in a sense the same. It's about who we see as our Creator or whatever being that we believe in, even though they all have different names and we use different languages.

Biami reached into Himself and took from His own essence and breathed life across the land and this became Nungeena-tya, the first feminine essence. He fell in love with this spirit and fertilised her seed with light. Then He sat, with sacred spear and boomerang, in front of the fire at His cave, in the most sacred place, waiting for the first born to come from Nungeena-tya, waiting for the first born to come from her womb.

The first-born was the Rainbow Serpent. This giant was actually two serpents that were joined together. On realising that they were joined to each other, the serpents began desperately trying to pull themselves apart. One became enraged at being attached to his brother, he was furious and his breath became fire and so anger was born. The second one, as he watched his brother suffering and struggling, cried tears for his brother's anguish and so compassion was born.

Immediately they were born, they started to tug and pull and tried to jerk apart, each trying to take control. They wove themselves around and in their thrashing formed the valleys, mountains, rivers and lakes that we know today. Anger's breath became so hot and the flames so fiery that one day his breath formed a ball of fire which floated to the sky to become Uri, the sun, as we know it today.[2]

Biami was so concerned for the suffering and destruction the serpent was causing that He tried desperately to pacify the first born by building His fire up higher and higher. And when it died down, He would build it up higher and higher; and when it died down again, He would build it up higher and higher again. Then one night a fireball from His fire floated into the sky to become, as we know it, Bahloo (the moon) — maker of girl babies. To this day Bahloo's fire dies down and dies out and disappears and then comes back to life again and again.

Biami realised the first born was destroying Creation as fast as it appeared. For as one serpent's breath was becoming so violently hot that it scorched everything, the other one's tears started to fill all the gullies, filling them more and more and more. So Biami, with great sadness, sent out two warriors — each armed with the sacred spear, the men's ceremonial spear — saying, 'You must slay the first born.' They did and, as the first born died, falling across the land, giving it all the colours as we know them today, death was born. All the colours went into the land to honour the Rainbow Serpent forever more.

Biami felt much pain in His heart, knowing that He had slain the first born and in doing so brought death upon His teaching place. He

Illustration 2. *The First Born.*

said to the rest of Creation, 'Whenever you see the breath of fire and the tears of the first born together, look up. Its spirit will be cast across the sky to remind us, for all of eternity, that it was the first born.' So what happens when you've got sun and rain together? A rainbow — the honouring of the first born.

The seed of Creation had already been spread from Biami so all the rest of Creation was born into the chaos of the first-born. In this teaching we didn't come from a serpent or a monkey. Biami gave us the breath of life, our Miwi, which is eternal. That is why we will be forever because we are His essence. We are also of the Earth, of Nungeena-tya that came from his essence. We all inherited anger and compassion from the first-born. And not just humanity either, but trees, animals and everything that is living struggles with this inheritance. We came after the serpent, and we were born with the serpent's emotions. So people who've spent their entire lives feeling guilty about being angry, you can now toss it because it's OK to be angry. It's what you do with that anger that either destroys or creates.

For example, if we accept that anger is part of who we are, when we recognise we are angry we have a chance to construct, dig, build, and carry heavy burdens with the strength that anger builds within us. Likewise too much compassion, and we drown in it. To have compassion is to give, tend and nurture, but in our perfectly imperfect state, this can leave too little for ourselves and resentment grows and we become angry. So compassion can be as destructive as anger, in a different kind of way. To become whole we have to constantly strive to balance anger with compassion. All the emotions were born as a direct result of these two emotions. From anger has come all the negative emotions and from compassion has emerged all the positive emotions and there lies our struggle for balance. Only when we can meet a stage in our lifetimes when our intimacy with all these emotions is complete can we then transcend them to become like our Creator. Some call this 'enlightenment'.

In the beginning everything that Biami created was big and to everything He gave lots of powers, extreme powers. He trusted that we would use the powers that He gave for the good but we didn't.

Something went terribly wrong. It started with the first-born but I don't know what happened or why. I've never been given an explanation.

Everything on this planet is therefore perfectly imperfect. In Creation, even the Creator can make mistakes. The Creator can think big, too big, because in the first world, everything was huge, giant — giant kangaroos without pouches, giant wombats, GIANT. Before the War of the Dreaming all was of a humungous size. Now that they're finding the skeletons of these giant animals, they're finding the proof. It's nice; I don't look so stupid anymore. They'll be finding giant kangaroos and giant wombats. And wait until they find the spirit turtle — that will really, really turn your hair curly. It was a doozey, that one. It looked like a crocodile with a shell — savage!

When Biami started Creation He said, 'I'll create all of my Creation and humanity will be the keepers of this. These people will live in harmony with all the animals and because this land is the womb of Creation, it will only feel the touch of gently padded feet, that's all it will ever feel because this is where Creation began.'

So He pulled from himself the Light and spread it across the land, and created animals that would live in harmony with the keepers of Creation. Leopards and tigers have softly padded feet; however, they are carnivores and could kill the keepers and so none of them live here. The wombat, the kangaroo, the emu, the koala, even the timid native tiger that is now extinct, all have gently padded feet and are unique to this country, this country alone. So we have been entrusted with something that is sacred.

The Story of How the Bunyip Came to Be

After a long time a clever man went on an Earth walk and he heard this sound – clop, clop, clop – and loved it. He looked for the sound and it was hoofed animals. He told them, 'I love the sound that your feet make.' They were pleased that he liked the sound and showed him how to make a pair of boots for his feet that made the same sound. He came home and wore them everywhere. Then Biami heard this clop, clop, clop and came to see where the noise was coming from because He had made it the lore/law that this sound would never be heard in the place of Creation. He saw the clever man and said, 'You know the lore/law — that this land will only ever feel the touch and hear the sound of gently padded feet. You are the keeper of my lore/law. Why have you got those on?'

The clever man replied, 'Well, they're mine and I like the sound they make and I'm keeping them on.'

Biami said, 'You have to take them off, because that's the lore/law.'

Again he refused. So Biami picked the clever man up and turned half of him into a hoofed animal. He threw him into the river saying, 'You can wear your shoes forever, but you can only ever wear them in the water.' And so the Bunyip came to be.

Biami built this planet from the purest essence of His love — when the clouds come down to the mountain it is Biami embracing Nungeena-tya. Our planet was to be a place of incredible love and beauty and all that is peaceful, a place where Biami could just be and walk among us and the rest of his Creation. This was the plan.

There are a number of places where Biami built fish traps and walked with his dogs. He came many times and walked the Earth and gave all his teachers the lore/law. He came and spent time with His children and His Creation. When He would come to visit, Biami favoured no group or tribe. He had no favourites but He continued to reward good deeds. When He came walking the Earth there were tribes who had very little and they would give Him the best or the last of what they had. For this He was grateful and so either then or the next time He visited, He would bring precious sweet or beautiful things from his own garden, from the Rivers of the Dreaming, as an offering to honour their generosity and goodness. He brought honey or sugar bag, manna (sugar creatures hanging from the trees), bush orange, native frangipani, macadamia, bunya bunya, midginberry, pipis, ground grape (found in semi-desert or desert regions), quinine, old man weed, gidgee tree and the grub that builds its nest in this tree. The grub spins a big bag of strands that can be the size of a football. Open the bag and empty the grubs and it can be used for burns. It is a natural antibiotic. He brought warrigal greens and many other gifts.[3]

Biami is the Creator and we get the Breath of Life, the Light of Life from Him. Some people call this essence, spirit, consciousness or soul. For my people it is called Miwi. Biami created this the teaching place where we come to journey towards spiritual enlightenment, but He also made us the keepers of Creation. So how can we pursue spiritual enlightenment on one hand and contribute to the destruction of the teaching place, Nungeena-tya, our mother, on the other? Who would stand by and watch their mother be bludgeoned and raped? We come from the Earth, Nungeena-tya, and she feeds us on her breast milk from the day we are born until the day we die. If we destroy our Mother, we destroy our very existence. So we are nurtured and we are cared for from birth to death by our Mother. This means everything that you take into your body, everything you wear and everything humanity makes comes from our Mother. So you are provided for. We have never left home really. This is the beginning of the understanding of the Oneness. The most important thing for us to first teach our children is about the Oneness and where they fit into Creation.

We have an obligation, as keepers of Creation, to our children. And they have an obligation to their children, and their children to their children. The obligation is that the first teaching they are given is about the Oneness of Creation and its importance to our survival. Sitting and telling is not enough. We have to live it every day and every moment of every day, even though ego has driven us to become disconnected from the Oneness.

Imagine a piece of fabric. Now pull a thread from this fabric and keep pulling threads. How long do you think it will be before that fabric weakens and completely unravels? If humanity removes itself from the Oneness we become weakened too. Helping children to recognise that they are part of the fabric, Oneness, will give them spiritual strength. If they have spiritual strength they can cope with anything; without it we condemn them to live in a world of spiritual lostness.

Chapter 3

THE DREAMING

In the Rivers of the Dreaming there are many islands, and many people, but there is only one teaching place where we come to learn two things, all Truth and all Knowledge, and our Earth is it. The Dreaming is how we came into Creation, how we came to be. We are living the Dreaming right now; we are part of the Dreaming. It's interwoven into every single thread in us and in what we do to or for each other. Everything that is living is part human; everything therefore is part of us. If we senselessly take life we are bleeding our own life away. If one thread is broken, we can unravel our own beingness and die.

Everything that's alive has spirit. We all come from the Earth; the Earth is our mother and nurtures us. We were all given the spirit-light by the Creator; so were the plants, the ants, everything. So as we hurt, destroy or dishonour Creation, we hurt, destroy and dishonour our own lives. It's like having an entire circle of candles all with different flames. These flames represent all that is living, the Oneness. All around the light is darkness. With lots and lots of candles there is lots and lots of light to see our way. If we go blowing out the candles, all we're left with is darkness. Can we stop ourselves putting out the lights?

All of us were given Miwi, the breath of life, by the Creator. It's important to look again at the lore/law and why Biami created humans. He created his Creation and then He created humanity to be the keepers of that Creation. Dishonour Creation and you dishonour the Creator. That's the way, that's the lore/law. If you are Hindu, Catholic, Protestant, Jewish, Muslim or of any religious belief and you go on your knees professing to love and honour your Creator and then turn around and wantonly destroy and disrespect his Creation, dishonouring your mother who provides for all your needs, then ask yourself, 'Am I a hypocrite?'

We are all part of Creation. We have a right to be here only as much as that tree out there has a right to be here, as the rivers have a right to be here and have a right to flow, as animals have a right to be here. In none of the languages in this country was there a word for thank you. How can you be thanked if you are part of the Oneness? What is there to thank? Everything has its place and its part in this Oneness.

The Oneness

What do I mean by Oneness? Imagine I have a large rock in my hand; see this as the Oneness of Creation, a big solid mountain that we are all part of. This gives us strength as well as protection, binding us together. Boss of self is part of understanding Oneness, part of the Dreaming. It is following your Miwi, your spirit path, and knowing your spirit is guiding you. As soon as you move to 'I should, I have to or I must' you are disconnected. When ego was born in humanity it developed very quickly. And with ego on board, rather than be part of that mountain, we said, 'We are better than this mountain. We'll just remove ourselves.' So we scraped ourselves away like a handful of ash from the mountain and at that moment we chose to separate from the Oneness of Creation. We are now a very powerful sickness for the planet; we have separated ourselves from the Oneness and when turbulence comes we are tossed aimlessly all over the place.

Humanity decided to inherit ego, big time. We then decided that Biami created the universe, the Earth just for us and that we would have dominion over the universe. We decided we could do whatever we liked to anything on this planet. So we separated ourselves from the rest of it. We are now superior so we can do what we want. We can get a puppy and give it to our children, let it be dragged around by the neck, only giving it food and water to shut its whining and whimpering up, because it's only a puppy after all and that's what you do with puppies. They keep the children from annoying you while you watch *The Bold and the Beautiful* or the footy, and because puppies are not like us they don't feel like we do. When we go on holidays we drop it at the pound because we will get a new one when we get back. We cage animals up in the smallest of cages because we like to have birds and animals and we can do that because we're two-legged and superior. Besides we don't have room for large cages — too messy, too much hard work.

Along with ego comes chaos. We are now in the time of chaos, moving through a war Dreaming track. Chaos has hit us and now along comes a BIG wind, Girrah, and whoosh — there we go, a handful of ash, gone, scattered into the universe, emotionally, spiritually and otherwise. There's the rest, still part of the Creation, still together, still anchored. There is absolutely no way that mountain can be blown away. But until we come back and recognise that we are only a very small part of a great Oneness — and we must honour that Oneness — we will remain scattered. Our separation will be at the cost of our very survival. That's where humanity has gone, and we can only blame ourselves. It's no good us sitting here and saying, 'Yes, but look at those before me. Look at what they've done, they started it. It isn't my fault. What can I do?' Whine, whine, and whine. It is not too late, you can change yourself but you can't change the others.

I will put our disconnection from the Oneness in terms of renting a house. Suppose you were told that in order to survive you would have to move house right now. This meant your very survival. So you go along to the local real estate agent and say, 'Well I've got to rent a house and I've got to bring along all my family.' The agent says, 'Yep, I've got one more house left to rent, one.' You're sooooo relieved. You go down with him and have a look at it, and from the outside it's the most spectacularly beautiful thing you've ever seen, you can't believe your luck. It has spacious gardens, genteel charm, made from beautiful old sandstone with verandahs all around — oooh, perfect. Then you walk inside. There's faeces all over the wall, syringes all over the floor, garbage, the carpets rotted in, there's mould growing out of the sink. You open the back door and there's rubbish everywhere, so much that you can barely move. Would you then go back to your house, your lovely, clean, comfortable, well cared for house, get a couple of friends and put all your stuff in the van and then move it down there? While you're getting the stuff out of the van, you get your friends to shove all the syringes and the faeces into a cupboard, and nail it shut. Over all the stuff that's been drawn on the wall, you hang a wall hanging. Then you say, 'Oh, bugger the backyard, it's too disgusting. We'll just nail the back door shut.' Then put your lovely Persian rug over the carpet that things have rotted into for years? Would you do that or would you clean it before you move in? If your answer is 'yes', why? You may say to me, 'But I cannot live with such filth.' I say, 'You didn't create this mess, why should you clean it up?' You reply, 'I can't raise my children in filth.' And there you go — there is your answer.

We want to leave our children a better world; we don't want them to live in filth because they're likely to die in it. So you must expand on that thinking. If you want a better world for your children this means clean water, clean rivers, clean oceans and trees to sit under. Biami said to take only what you need and not what you greed and there will always be plenty. So what do we do, we take on the personality of a centipede and are greedy for a hundred pairs of shoes. Then it begins to snowball and suddenly our arse develops a multiple personality disorder and we greed a hundred pairs of knickers, one for each personality. We must have two TVs, two cars and it never ends. We have lost control to greed and what do our children inherit: the rubbish of our greed.

That is why I try to teach about the Oneness. I try to instil that all creatures deserve to be here. All life is precious. It is important to feed the birds, as we are only a thread woven through a fabric and you have to start somewhere. I try to teach children that trees have feelings. I try to instil into them that the food they don't eat can be fed to other creatures whose habitat we have overtaken, so they can continue their species. I stand by my belief that it is better to feed birds white bread, if that is all that I have, if that will keep them alive. I want my grandchildren to be fully aware that they are only a small part of a great Oneness and a very small part at that. It is their first lesson in humility and their first step towards wisdom.

The Story of the Giant Green Ant and the Golden Sunset Spider

Now in the Dreaming, before the war of the Dreaming, Biami was confident to give all He created great powers and great size — giant kangaroos and giant wombats, and so on. Everything was big. I'm going to tell you a story about two very important creatures of the Dreaming. You can see this as a teaching or you can see it just as a great story that you can tell your children or your grandchildren. Either way this is one of the most important stories I'll ever tell anybody.

It is about a giant green ant of the Dreaming. Now this lad was absolutely beautiful. He was like no green that is on this planet today. He was a real cutie and everywhere he went everything else would go, 'Wow! Look at that gorgeous colour. Beautiful!'

One day green ant was walking over by a still water pond and he happened to look down and he went, 'Gorgeous all right! I'm a hunk and a half. You know I'm beautiful.'

Then of course he started to walk differently, because he was beautiful. Finally, when anything he thought was less beautiful came near him, he'd go, 'Out of my way, ugly!'

He spent all his time posing in the pond looking at how beautiful he was and vanity was born. When anyone or anything stood up to him, he started to spit a poison enzyme. Remember they were giants. The mucus that he sent out destroyed many things; nothing would grow, nothing would live. It was absolutely lethal — forever. All ants on the planet today have an enzyme they use to break down matter. So all ants now carry something from the first one. This is one lore/law.

The next important creatures of the Dreaming were the golden sunset spiders — deadly lads. They would weave absolutely beautiful golden webs, glorious these webs were. They would spin and spin these beautiful webs. Everything that came past said, 'Aren't they beautiful webs? What gorgeous, gorgeous webs!'

The more people said they were beautiful the harder the golden sunset spiders spun, until the webs were perfect. They wanted them more and more perfect so people would keep coming past and saying, 'You're so clever, look at those beautiful webs!'

One day a golden spider turned around and said, 'It is actually. This is perfect. In fact this is the most beautiful thing on this planet.'

under the quandong tree 21

And so ego was born. As their egos became bigger and bigger the spiders made the webs more and more intricate until everything that they covered began to suffocate.

So you had the golden sunset spider suffocating and the giant green ant poisoning and killing. The clever people, that Biami had made the keepers of the lore/law, came to Him in his cave and said, 'Biami all these terrible things are happening.'

So Biami went to the golden sunset spiders and said, 'Golden sunset spiders, your webs are beautiful but everything that you cover suffocates. You can't do that because everything that is living is part of you. As you kill it, so too does part of you die.'

The golden sunset spiders stood their ground with Biami saying, 'Our webs are so beautiful they should cover this entire place and if you come near us we will cover and suffocate you.' By then their egos were so big that they actually thought that they could do over the Creator, deadly lads.

Biami realised that you must have wisdom before you have power. He went to the giant green ants and said to their community, 'Giant green ants you are part of everything else. You can't do this even though, yes, you are beautiful. Everything has as much right to be here as you.'

The leader said, 'We're beautiful so we deserve this whole place to ourselves, our kind, and if you come near us Biami we will destroy you.'

Biami went back to His cave and, knowing these creatures had power without wisdom, He had a real dilemma on his hands. It wasn't just these two that were off their faces, it was many, many more. So He called all the goodies together and said, 'We have to stop them because they will destroy the teaching place.' His heart was really sad but so began the first war of the Dreaming. (In many belief systems there are similar stories to this one although not another, that I know of, about a 'war'. In one it is known as the great flood. At the end of the day it is all only interpretation.)

Biami gave special powers to the goodies He had called together. He gave one of His clever men, Wahwee — the water spirit — powers to rain and rain and rain and rain some more. So it rained and rained. Wahwee was furious in his letting go of the water. Finally all over the Dreaming tracks and out in the cosmos they fought battles.

There are many places over this continent where these battles were fought, where many goodies gave their lives or were caught in the fighting. One of these places is Mootwingee National Park out near Broken Hill in New South Wales. There you'll see a sacred women's waterhole where all the stone is grey but for one black stone. This black stone is the pregnant woman sitting over the waterhole, the giver of new life. Up on another ridge you'll see a warrigal stepping, like he's about to go somewhere, from under the wing of an eagle poised in flight. All turned to stone. Then there's the black-headed carpet snake that I think is one of the songlines up there. If you just stand and step back you'll even see snake scales and where his head's been broken. So the spirits of the good fighters are contained in these stones. That's why stone is not dead – it's got a living pulse force. Now Mootwingee is a sacred Dreaming place/track. If you want to connect to the spirit within, go there with honour and respect and it will honour and respect you. Go to the Koori people out there, ask their permission. They are strong in their beliefs to honour and keep this place.

So this terrible war was fought and the goodies won. Otherwise we wouldn't be sitting here and I wouldn't be telling you this. The giant green ant and the golden sunset spider were put to sleep under all the mud and the rain, for eternity. Then Biami said, 'Where the giant green ants of the dreaming sleep there will be sixty-six markers around these places. All the men of this line and these tribes will forever ensure that they are kept asleep under all this Earth, never to be disturbed. If they rise up they could destroy mankind and the teaching place. Here there are 116 markers where the golden sunset spider sleeps. All you men of this tribe will forever more keep them asleep, by performing ceremonies. Those who trespass here will be under the lore/law of death. They are never to be disturbed. You will perform this dance and ceremony and keep them here forever.'

A man stepped forward and asked, 'Biami, what if we forget the dance, what if we forget the ceremony?'

He replied, 'To you men I leave the udarrki (better known as the didgeridoo). It will be given to a male reaching wanai. He will have his personal totem here and he will fill in the story, his journey. These instruments will be taboo to women. There within the udarrki will be the spirit of the udarrki that will forever dictate the dance so it will never be lost. To you women, I leave you the sacred singing sticks of wattle, black wattle. They will be given to a female on reaching wanai. They too will have their tribal totem here, their personal totem there and they will fill in their story. This wood is taboo to men, they will never touch this.'

These are women's ceremonial singing sticks, not to be confused with clap sticks. They are power sticks. When the white people first came, every house was built of daub and black wattle and this wattle was almost completely eradicated.

The markers around the resting places of the giant green ants and the sleeping places of the golden sunset spiders are significant for the men of certain tribes and all their descendants and identify their responsibility. Everyone who travelled around could see these markers and know that these were sacred places, the resting place of the giant green ants or the golden sunset spiders. The markers identified the spirits that lie there and that have to be kept there. There are many things that can cause upheaval in a tribe and it can be very difficult for them to find their way back. Men know about the markers. I don't know the markers, because only men can identify them. But I do know they are all negative places around the globe. There are many places and every single one has their own identifying marker, be it in England in a different language, in South America in a different language, or in North America in a different language.

When the early settlers of this country started to spread their way around Australia the old people would sit them down and say, 'No no, don't go there. You must hear this story. It is important you must hear this story. No, no, no, you must hear this story.' They would tell them that the giant green ant or the golden sunset spider sleeps there. To their detriment the settlers associated these teachings with 'Humpty Dumpty' or 'Hickory Dickory Dock'. To them it was just childish mythology told by sub-humans. And early anthropologists were simply fascinated by these little stories. Well, cop this: we call one the sleeping place of the golden sunset spider, and you call it asbestos. Asbestos suffocates and people die of suffocation. The other one we call the sleeping place of the giant green ant of the Dreaming, and you call it uranium. Uranium destroys absolutely everything that it touches.

Now there's a place in the Northern Territory called Coronation Hill. Many of you will have heard of this place. The lore/law says this is the sleeping place of the leader of the giant green ants, and if he's ever released there will be absolutely no hope for this planet. Remember, within the Rivers of the Dreaming there are many islands and many people; there is but one teaching place where we come to learn two things, all truth and all knowledge. This is it. Whatever happens, we don't need uranium. We can harness the energy of the Sun that will not hurt anybody. We do not need uranium. It causes destruction and greed. We export uranium to make money but who can eat money? Who's going to be alive when there's nothing else? I've never ever been political, because I can't be political, it's not my role. However if Coronation Hill was opened up and mined I believe it would be all our responsibilities to put our lives on the line to prevent this from happening. If we don't there will be no future, there will be no teaching place.

Dreaming Tracks[4]

As a result of the first war of the Dreaming we were left with positive and negative Dreaming tracks. These are spirit tracks. Dreaming tracks are not to be confused with songlines. Positive Dreaming tracks are light lines and they come from the light of the Creator, the light that we all have. I have been told some people call these ley lines. There are Dreaming tracks like realms and there are negative forces. The universe is threaded with Dreaming tracks, as is Earth. The Rivers of the Dreaming are all the Dreaming tracks of the Universes. There is infinite time and Earth time. A Dreaming track is a track of light, Biami's breath light. And a negative Dreaming track[5] is where it has been damaged by bugeenge or where right and wrong warred and wrong has won. Sometimes wrong wins; this is good for us, it makes us appreciate right. It is a good teaching as it makes us aware what wrong intention can do. It makes us grateful when we receive justice and it helps instil in our Miwi the need to be just. For all the wrong reasons — to protect someone we love or to get something we want — we often resort to injustice.

The positive Dreaming tracks are there to come up through our Miwi to help us and protect us and remind us that help is at hand. Walking or sitting in a thinking place on a positive Dreaming track is like a Christian walking a difficult dark path, without light, holding the hand of Jesus; it's like a Muslim walking down a difficult and dangerous path holding the hand of Allah; or like a Buddhist holding the hand of Buddha. A Dreaming track is not about any kind of religion or belief. It is about being encompassed in the light of the Creator — the pure goodness of compassion. A negative Dreaming track is created when one dishonours pure light and compassion from any path. We, Earthbound humans, create negative Dreaming tracks by our greed, resentment, anger, ego, arrogance and ignorance and by our need to own the Creator and the Creation.

The Earth moves to different Dreaming tracks about every 5000 years. Over the first 2000 years we shed the layers of the last Dreaming track before we reveal the true essence of the next. Then for 1500 to 1700 years, I think, it is in our consciousness. Some of us shed and reveal and some of us never do. Each Dreaming track carries an essence which is part of the essence of the Creator. All the Dreaming tracks are of self-knowledge and self-consciousness and because we have the essence of the Creator within us, we have the potential to reveal characteristics of divine energy.

The Dreaming track the Earth is moving onto now is higher spiritual consciousness. For the last 5000 years the Earth has been on the dreaming track of physical knowledge. We have advanced in the sense of this knowledge. We are given the opportunity to absorb the essence from Biami but there are pitfalls. We have within us the will to do or not to do and there is our intention.

For example, imagine if you were sitting on the Dreaming track of justice and the family was with you. Say you were Westerners, Christian or no faith, and you're on this Dreaming track and you absorb its essence. It impregnates every fibre of your being. Now imagine on that same place camping right beside you are some Palestinians, and their ten-year-old and your ten-year-old are playing together as friendly children do. Down in a sacred place there is a sacred Wandjina and you are walking by in the bush and you see your child destroy it and the other child is only laughing. You say nothing but it is discovered and the Westerners say it must have been the

Palestinians because your child said it was the other child. You know the truth, but do you deny the truth out of shame, loyalty, love or fear? Remember you are in a justice Dreaming track — you carry it for eternity and you burden your child with it as well. This is how easy it is to do the wrong thing.

On the Dreaming track of physical knowledge one of the major tests was to see what we could handle, how we would grow in totality. What has happened is the more knowledge we have acquired of the physical, the more 'clever' we have become in our mind's delusions. Arrogance, ego and narcissism have taken over until many of us believe that we are greater than our Creator. If you don't believe me, look at the theory on evolution — our Creator has been cast out altogether and our faith in ourselves as spirits has gone. Instead of being the keepers of Creation we have become the blight.

Because of the war of the Dreaming there are positive and negative dreaming tracks. The planet is now covered with negative Dreaming tracks where bugeenge grows and positive Dreaming tracks where healing grows. The spirit will never become bugeenge on positive tracks.

Visitors to Australia often experience a connection or awareness. It may be the first time in their lives they have such an intense awakening of a greater consciousness. It comes from absorbing the spiritual essence of the Dreaming track of Creation. Perhaps it's feeling the heartbeat of the Mother. The Dreaming tracks are very strong here, in Australia. I've compared the power of the Dreaming tracks here with the power in many parts of the world and the closest that I have come to that same kind of power is the Rockies in Canada. It's almost the same. I haven't been all over the world; however, I've been in enough places to compare the energy. And remember, I can see the tracks.

There are very, very powerful points, energy points around the Earth where the Dreaming tracks meet in webs, be they negative or positive. The following examples are all positive Dreaming tracks but there are lots of places, so I'll mention some of the most powerful and significant I know. Take into account that I know very little. These tracks meet up in a super force at places like Uluru which is the most powerful, Wave Rock (Western Australia), parts of the Kimberleys,

Obiri Rock (Northern Territory), Bangalow, Murwillumbah, Point Plummer (Port Macquarie) and a place near South West Rocks where Biami's son was killed a long time ago.

The most powerful Dreaming track down my end of the country runs close to the surface in a place called Kangaroo Valley. This place is a source of incredible spiritual power for anyone who seeks solace or grounding or stillness within themselves. Perhaps you have been to Kangaroo Valley. Did you have a bad experience? I doubt it. Goolooga down south, known as the mother of the stars, is on the same Dreaming track. So is a place called Wuuluumbin (Mount Warning), one of the most powerful and significant for us now and for the planet's future. This is where the eighth sister sleeps. Some people now say Wuuluumbin is a men's place. RUBBISH. Yes, there are men's ceremonial sites up there, as there are women's. However, the very top of Wuuluumbin is for everyone because everyone has a right to be where Uri (the Sun) first kisses this land with her blessing every morning. Over eons of time many have climbed up to receive this blessing from her. The 'men's place' statement was probably started by some lad who wants to grow huge gurra (balls) to impress. Whoever he is, I say, go very carefully. No doubt what I say to you will have little effect, but don't bring the lore/law down on yourself because you may find yourself gurraless!

If you are on Wuuluumbin at dawn, where the Sun first touches this continent, and if you are in the mist and see the spirit of the Rainbow Serpent swirling, it means you have chosen to come back to play a significant part in the changing path of humanity, or the changing of this planet. If you are thinking of going to Wuuluumbin with real sorrow in your heart or just after you have lost someone who's died, don't go! Don't go! If you do, when you get there all the emotional pain you have within could be exacerbated a thousand-fold and destroy you. If you go with a dream, like with a vision, it too could be magnified a thousandfold. So be very, very careful. Your life may never be the same once you've been to Wuuluumbin. And please take your shoes off there. It's similar to going to Uluru; it's on the same Dreaming track.

Point Plummer near Port Macquarie is also powerful. Be careful if you go there without the pill! Point Plummer is baby spirit. I'm telling you, if you go there, baby spirits will follow you to the ends of the Earth! They hook into you and they won't let up. If people want babies, they go to Point Plummer, they swim in the water there and they have babies. Even if you say, 'Oh well, you know I've been on the fertility program', still, go to Point Plummer. You've got nothing to lose; it's free.

There are other spots around that are very powerful, especially on the top of hills where you've got a 360-degree view. That's where the ceremonies were held to call Biami, because you can access the eight directions of the Universe.

Feeling and recognising the power of these Dreaming tracks has nothing to do with people's skin colour and it's got nothing to do with religion either. It's got to do with what our Miwis are picking up. Mental institutions could have been built in Kangaroo Valley. Prisons could have been built on top of Mount Warning. These institutions should have been built in healing places rather than places that will manifest more bugeenge. Bugeenge means no good, negative energy, bad.

Dreaming tracks are purely power, spirit and the lore/law. The lore/law is back. The Dreaming tracks carry the lore/law of Creation and the lore/law is very clear. Number one, you're boss of self. You can only take responsibility for yourself, nobody else. Ego, greed, intolerance, love and so on, all of these are our opponents. With the energy coming back into Nungeena-tya, she is awakening our Miwis.[6]

People who are on a vision quest, a spiritual journey, need to go to places of spiritual significance, often on positive Dreaming tracks. There are always teachers but these are not always two-legged or four-legged; they could have feathers or appear out of rock. Dogs, for example, are among the great teachers. Dogs are teachers of unconditional love; we might starve, beat, neglect and abuse them and still every time we appear they love and greet us. We are often too blinded to see they are great teachers. But note this also about human teachers.

Keep in mind, everything has been created on this planet with the essence of the first born, and so we are perfectly imperfect. If you seek perfection, then you're in the wrong joint. I don't know why we seek perfection because on this planet there is absolutely nothing that is perfect. So when you're on a vision quest you go to the places of spiritual significance where the light is indescribable and you just get encapsulated in this light. Then you are able to break free from the layers of sediment that have built up from being human on this planet — sediment caused by our very imperfections, for example greed, envy, vanity, ego etc. Remember we carry lifetimes of sediment into each new life hoping to deal with it and grow from it.

Some women have come with me to the 'Beach of Souls'. At this beach there is a sacred pool — a Miwi cleansing pool — that remains totally hidden until the teachers know when it is open. After immersing yourself in the sacred pool you re-enter the womb of Nungeena-tya where you have the opportunity to leave behind layers of your sediment to be absorbed by her. All that no longer serves any purpose in your life — for example, resentment of elements of your childhood, negative attitudes toward your parents, betrayal of your love and trust by someone, grief, loss and so on — can be shed. Sometimes I have shown women the 'Singer of the Spirit Turtle' (that comes to collect the Miwis/spirits) and even though they may have visited there many times they have not seen the 'Singer' until it was pointed out to them.

We have to let go and just 'be' to realise that we are already on the Dreaming track, our vision quest. It is only our humanness that blinds us. Hopefully after many lifetimes we will find our first sparks of wisdom. We all need our thinking place — and we all need to go and immerse ourselves in a Dreaming track at some stage in order to follow our path. Now some of you will immediately think I mean a positive dreaming track. NO. There are many, many people who have chosen to come back in this life and spend it on a negative Dreaming track. This is because they are there to temper the negative effect of these Dreaming tracks. They are beacons.

Positive Dreaming tracks have started to lose energy over the last few centuries because of the destruction of Nungeena-tya, Mother Earth, by us. Positive Dreaming tracks are incredibly powerful. People have spiritual experiences like you'll never believe and it doesn't matter whether you are Indigenous or not or what religion you are or what socio-economic background you come from. Some people will go, 'Oh this is not really happening,' and others will embrace it.

It doesn't matter who you are as everyone has a Miwi and that's what is on its journey. This Miwi — some people call it gut instinct or intuition — directs your journey. It will pick up on places. It will tell you, 'No, no; yes, yes; back off; go here; go there' — and that's your journey. Always follow this and you'll never make a mistake in your life. If you do make mistakes, do me a favour, you a favour and everyone a favour — please let every mistake you make be your own. When you make a mistake, look for the teaching in that mistake so you'll grow. When people say, 'You should do that, you must do this,' go back to your Miwi (gut instinct, intuition). This needs to direct you.

Women need to develop their knowing. We're supposed to do everything now from the brain and from rationalism, which is not working. Maybe you have been on a men's site or somewhere and you've been walking and your Miwi goes, 'No, no, no, bad, bad, bad, danger, danger, danger!' You start to feel sick and uncomfortable. Move off it! Just get out of there! There are other places you can go and you just know these are the most amazing places and they are usually on a positive Dreaming track. It is the Dreaming tracks that influence your Miwi. I probably could draw all the Dreaming tracks. It would take a long time but maybe it's something that I should really think about doing, because I know where a lot of them are. However it could defeat the purpose of encouraging women to actually find their Miwi journey and discover for themselves where they get most power.

Dreaming tracks go everywhere. One in New South Wales, a very powerful, positive Dreaming track starts in the ocean, near Ulladulla; it comes in from the ocean, rising, rising, rising, rising, right up through Kangaroo Valley (*see Illustration 3*). Then it goes right down deep and comes closer to the surface at Point Plummer. It again comes near the surface — but not right up — at Burrell Bulli (Sugarloaf Mountain). Then it goes down and comes up again when it hits Mount Warning. Where it comes right to the surface you feel the most power. It goes deep down in the Earth, then it comes up really close to the surface and that's where you get the full influence, completely.

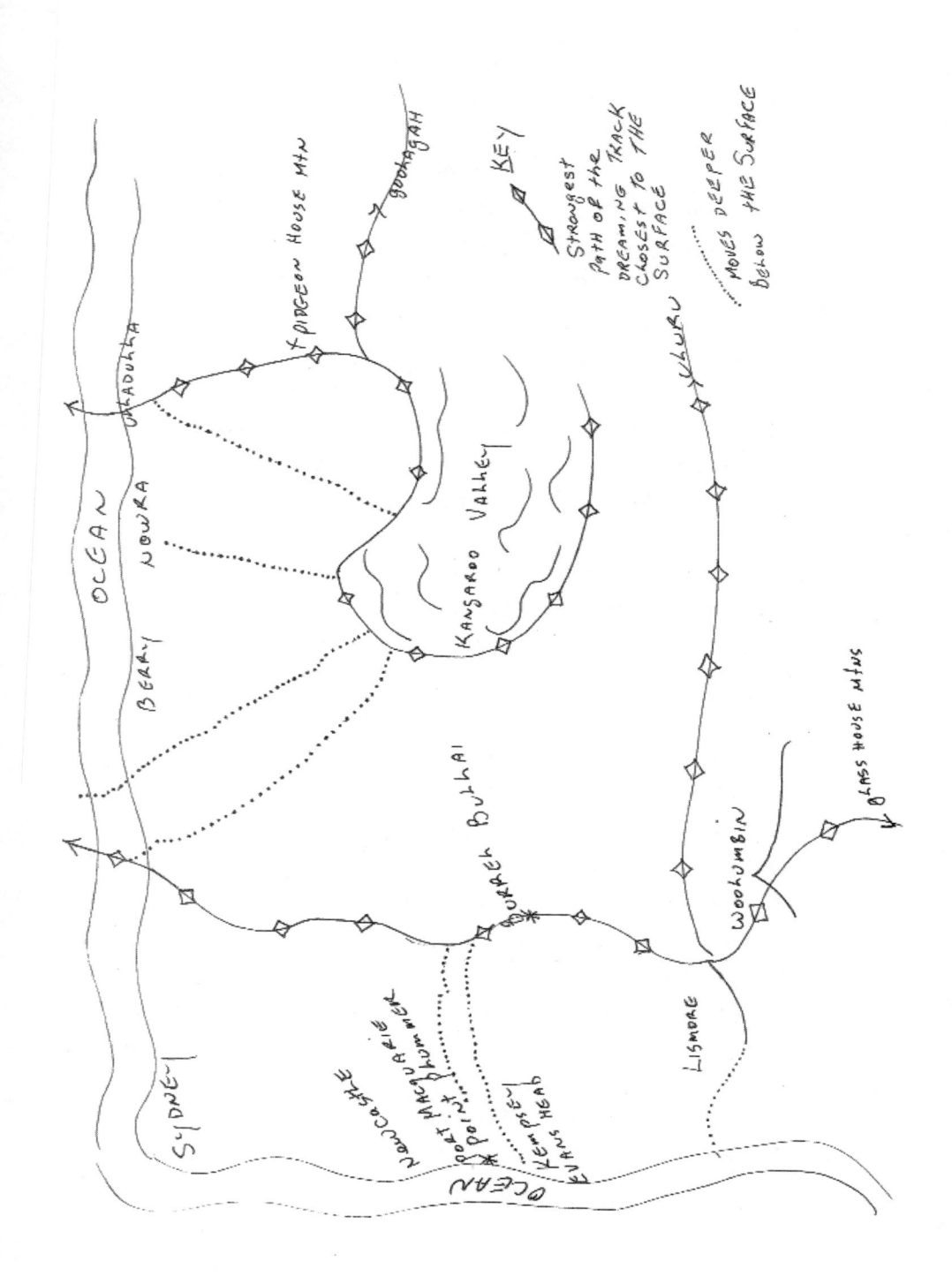

Illustration 3. A Dreaming Track.

Some people can't handle the energy because it vibrates all the way through you and it scares people because it's so raw. That's part of the reason, I think, why the biggest Buddhist temple in the Southern Hemisphere, Nan Tien at Berkeley near Wollongong — and all the artists' galleries — are there in Wadi Wadi country. They are connecting to the track from Kangaroo Valley. This powerful Dreaming track again comes quite close to the surface near Wollongong and cuts across into Picton and swings back away behind Campbelltown.

There are negative Dreaming tracks in this country and all over the world. They exist where a really bad battle was lost during the first war of the Dreaming and the negative essence of destruction has permeated the area and settled there. It was really bad there. There are a couple of places within New South Wales where there are strong negative Dreaming tracks. The people who live in the towns on these tracks aren't bugeenge. They don't necessarily have negative energy, but their energy is needed there in order to repair the damage to the Dreaming track. They are sponge beacons who absorb the negative energy and change it to light. This can take millions of years. The other people chose to be there, they have come back to the area for a reason. Remember, we choose our lives, we choose our parents, we choose our teachings and we choose where to be.

Governments, none of them black governments, have built prisons and mental institutions all along the negative Dreaming tracks — amazing! And major highways run on the Trading Routes — unbelievable! The city of Goulburn, in New South Wales, is on a negative Dreaming track which goes around by Yass and back. People who go through Goulburn say, 'Oh, Goulburn is terrible. It's really cold, it's really miserable.' They are on their way to the snow. Think about it! But still they say, 'Goulburn is miserable, the wind goes right through you, I can't stand it.' And it's just that you're not supposed to be there. It manifests in the physical but we are not rational about it until we stop and realise, 'It's so awful and cold here and yet I'm on my way to the snow where it's freezing.' There are prisons, mental institutions and the police academy in Goulburn. All there in

Goulburn, oozing. So when you go through Goulburn put ochre everywhere. Go through painted up and as you're driving through and people at the traffic lights stare and glare at you just go, 'G'day,' and keep going. Use ochre, burn incense in the car, make the kids hold it out the windows, do anything at all to get you through there.

Another Dreaming pocket on a negative Dreaming track is a place called Weston, at the back of Maitland, between Newcastle and Cessnock. In the last fifteen years there have been a number of really bad deaths there — murders. I think it has become a negative Dreaming pocket either because of massacres or more likely after the first war of the Dreaming. Around that area is coal and coal is bugeenge spirit — it is deadly. It gives off a deadly gas.

There are a number of negative Dreaming tracks but these are the two strongest that I know of down this end of the country. People who aren't supposed to be there can be negatively influenced on these tracks. We go there because we don't listen to our Miwis anymore. We still go to places when our gut intuition, our Miwi goes, 'No, no, get out, get out'! We say, 'Gosh, I'm being really silly,' and we stay there. It's the worst thing we can do. Our spirits, our Miwis, are always having to battle with our computer (our intellect). Our Miwis need to direct our computer to bring them into balance. What we've done is pushed our Miwi down to shut it up and now we're using only our intellect. However, if we listen to our Miwis our way will never detour far off our journey wherever we are.

You have to learn to be guided by your Miwi. Suppose you're sent to a meeting and you're told this is a very, very important meeting. You get up and your Miwi says, 'No, no, no, don't go, don't go!' If you go what you'll find is that you weren't meant to be there. So just say, 'Well my Miwi says no, sorry.' When I used to work and I was told to go somewhere if my Miwi said 'No' I just said 'No'. But people still told me that I had to go. 'No,' I'd say, 'I'm not going. I'm not going up that high building. If I was meant to be right on that top floor I'd have feathers and I don't have any feathers.' They'd call me eccentric or whatever but I'd listen to my Miwi. It can very well save your life, listening to your Miwi.

Trust your Miwi to know where you should and shouldn't be. Under the teachings first you learn about every single inch of your tribal country. You learn how the rivers come to be, how this stone comes to be, how this mountain comes to be. You get to know her as well as you know your parents or your children because your prime parent is Nungeena-tya. Your other parent is your nurturer in early life to start you off on your teachings. Nungeena-tya is your prime parent because without her where would you be? Dead. She provides everything that we have, from our clothes to our food. So you get to know all of that first. You know your mother, backwards, forwards and sideways. You learn all of your life — you go out just like a ripple in a pond. You know where the positive and negative Dreaming tracks are. You know where your ceremonial sites are. So you know where to avoid, where to go, where to get spiritual fulfilment and so forth.

The Story of Burradahn, Son of Biami

Biami and his army defeated the destructive creatures of the Dreaming but He could not destroy the essences they left behind. The essences of greed, envy and vanity and many of our other opponents remained. So there was still chaos among the keepers of Creation, as in the following story of Nimbin.

Biami looked down and saw that people were forgetting the lore/law, the teaching. Even the sacred teachers were overtaken by greed, ego and vanity and He was very concerned because there had already been the war of the Dreaming. This left Him very sad for to watch what you have created slowly decay before your eyes is heart-wrenching. He said to His son Burradahn, 'I have to send you down to the teaching place to remind the teachers and all on the teaching place of the law/lore.'

He knew He could trust Burradahn to do this for Him. So Burradahn came down and started to walk among the people. He was the essence of humility. They saw this and were not afraid and started to listen again.

One of the teachers, a clever man entrusted with the teachings, became envious of the people's love and trust in Burradahn and envy was born. Envy walked hand in hand with jealousy and anger and then malice thought he would get in the act too. They walked beside the clever man, taunting him, saying, 'No-one follows you like this, no-one loves you like this, nobody treats you as you should have been treated. You have endured

under the quandong tree

all the hard work and suffering and Burradahn has taken all the glory.' In his mind he had been robbed.

The envious teacher had been using his knowledge to control and exploit and had elevated himself to Biami on Earth. Now he was being ignored and he did not like this. So he became a wirrinun — a lore/law breaker. He waited and waited and watched Burradahn and waited for his chance. Burradahn fell asleep in a place near the sea. This wirrinun had plotted to kill Burradahn but was too afraid to do it himself and cowardice was born. So he used his apprentice saying, 'While Burradahn is sleeping you sneak up with this spear and kill him.' The apprentice did this. Then, realising what they had done, they both ran and hid.

The next morning they went to hide the body of Burradahn. They snuck back but there was no body. Burradahn had gone. As they stood there puzzled, they heard a mighty roar from the Rivers of the Dreaming, and the land shook as Biami began to walk towards them and every step shook the Earth for Biami was angry. He roared, 'How dare you kill my son whose essence was humility and who only walked a gentle walk among you at my request.' The wirrinun and his apprentice fled in fear and shame, all eyes upon them.

Biami reached down and ripped the mighty tree that his son had died under from the ground with His bare hands. And He wept and where His tears dropped the stones turned from sandstone to white quartz. He wept for His son, His Creation, the wirrinun and for humanity. He reached down and picked up stones, still wet with His tears, and offered them with compassion. Even in His suffering, He offered, 'Here are my tears. I give them to you to remind you I too endure suffering.' As He gave Burradahn back his life, He held the tree high above His head and declared, 'From this day this tree will be known as the tree of life.'

So the mighty fig tree became the sacred tree of life. Now all fig trees are sacred. They signify rebirth and renewal. If you want guidance or seek change, go and sit under a fig tree and ask. You can take the first step in developing a relationship and understanding with the tree spirits.

Where Biami ripped the tree from the Earth was close to the sea. All the sandstone became white quartz which was flung far and wide in the ocean and embedded in the mountains and Earth. Where the tree had been was a great gaping hole filled with this white stone. He picked up a piece of the white stone and declared that this stone and this place would be sacred and the stone will be known as the healing stone. From the South to the North Coast of New South Wales white quartz was given to the people as a healing stone.

In his wrath Biami went after the wirrinun to punish him. He found him and turned him to Earth and the wirrinun is now a mountain. There he will sit for eternity, contemplating his terrible deed of betraying the trust of his Creator.

Then Biami turned to his apprentice who pleaded for his life, saying, 'My teacher made me do it.'

Biami said, 'You are boss of self, you take responsibility for your own deeds.' And with a wave of His hand the apprentice was also turned to Earth and became a hill. The wirrinun is under stone near the town of Nimbin and the apprentice is under the hill nearby. Their bugeenge energy lives on. Women do not go there.

It is clear in this teaching that if you are not confident in yourself, true to self, insecurity and fear take over. Then envy creeps in and malice takes over — and malice can cause such destruction, such bugeenge that it reverberates through the Rivers of the Dreaming forever. It is so potent because it is destruction with intent; it is not just anger. The teaching tells us never to betray the trust given to us, the sacred trust of holding the lore/law. If we make a sacred commitment of holding the lore/law that is what we must do for we know what the consequence will be if we don't. We are reminded that we are boss of self, we are born boss of self, we walk our journey boss of self and we die boss of self. Remember, let every mistake you make in this life be your own mistake and not somebody else's for we get our truest teachings from learning from our mistakes.

You must know about every single thing and its purpose in order to honour it. This is what I mean about the Oneness. Everyday we say, 'I don't get validated enough. I'm a person too. Can't you see I'm a human being? Can't you see I'm a woman? I'm not just a mother, wife, driver, cleaner.' We really resent the fact that we have all these labels put on us. We want to be seen as the spirit, as the spiritual being that we are. So we get pissed off. We get angry if people don't validate us because we all need to be validated. This is not an ego thing. We all need to be validated in order to grow, for our light to grow. So do all other living things. Everybody knows that the more you put someone down, the more you shove them down, the more that person shrinks. It's not just the physical self. That doesn't really matter — that's like an old skirt. You throw it away and you get a new one later. But the Miwi itself actually shrinks. It becomes weak and the dahwee[7] weakens and bugeenge can get through. So everything has to be validated, everything that's been created. You can't expect to be honoured and validated as a unique spiritual being on a journey if you're not prepared to do the same for everything else that is living.

Knowing all the lore/law and all the stories and all the instructions that are etched into every single part of the landscape, in every single thing that exists even in us, is part of the honouring. Everything, everything that has been created, has been created for a reason. For example, the fig tree is the tree of life and so signifies rebirth and renewal, yet people cut them down. The bunya bunya is another sacred tree — the sacred tree of knowledge. There's one in Central Australia, the yarrin, the sacred tree of death to remind us we are only mortal.

The essence of Oneness is there in the she-oak. When the male she-oak turns brown and starts to throw his spore and looks dead, he's just fertile, very fertile. They give off all these spores that blow on the wind and the female in her desire catches them. It's simple enough. You look at the she-oaks and think, 'Ah, they've all gone brown.' But Kooris look at them and think, 'All the big fish, the salmon, they've come in to do their Dreaming. They're on their journey. The mutton birds are on their endurance trek. Don't eat oysters now because they are having their own Dreaming.' So because all the big fish (including sharks) come in close to shore to have their Dreaming, you get the real good fishing time — but also a dangerous swimming time at dawn and dusk. And when the beach cherry is in fruit you can't touch the pipis, or the concles because that's the time of their Dreaming.

Learning the lore/law is more than just reading this book. It's about understanding that every single thing that has come into Creation has its story, its power and its essence. Everything must have its Dreaming without interference from us.

There are at least eight seasons. Some mobs have ten but it's generally eight. They're not seasons like you might know them, they're Dreamings. The traditional word is gadtjirrka. There are some major and some shared Dreamings. The spring Dreaming is a big one. In some teachings the world was created in six days and on the seventh day the Creator rested. This was a very quick Creator. Ours was done in Koori time.

The last week in September and the first two weeks in October, these twenty-one days are the Creation dreaming and they're incredibly celebrated with very high-powered ceremonies. Depending on what songline you are, everyone has a responsibility for certain Dreamings and singing up those Dreamings, their reproduction and continuance towards eternity. It's a ceremony of honouring and being part of the Oneness.

So there you go, every month there is a different Dreaming, fertility Dreaming. They're all different depending on what tribe and when their Dreamings occur. But the last week in September and the first two weeks in October are vital. That's when you should celebrate all of Creation and throw off your clothes and be at one. Get out on the beach and go 'la la la' like a 'pig in the city'.

Down on the south coast of New South Wales there's the bush rice Dreaming, which is very, very important. Bush rice provides food for five to six months of the year and it doesn't stop. The grain can be stored. Then there's the gidgin and all the berry fruit Dreamings. Out in the desert there's the quandong Dreaming and the bush banana Dreaming that shares its Dreaming with the quandong Dreaming. These go for a long time.

You see everything is linked to the Oneness. The more you learn about the whole of Creation, the Creator and each other, the more you become connected to the Oneness of Creation. And the more you honour Creation, the more honourable you become.

I don't care what colour anybody is. I couldn't give a rat's arse about what religion people follow. There are people in this world who I have met who I don't like at all. However I love humanity, I love humanity because of the light, the infinite divine light that people carry. I can't say, 'Oh my, I just loooove everybody' because some people I have met have been absolute deadshits. But I think there is hope for us and I think overall we are capable of great, great things. We need to come all the way back down to self and look at this. We need each other, we need each other's light. If we dishonour the other's light then we don't have any light to move by. So remember, everything that is living has a light and for every light we take, snuff out or destroy it is one light less to guide us along our own treacherous path in the dark.

Everything has a right to be. Everything has a purpose to be. I am not saying go into your backyard and dig up a nest of ants and take it inside, not at all. What I'm saying is, what do you know about ants? What do you really know about ants? They come in and eat your sugar and they get in your cupboard. When they get on your legs they bite you. They are only pests. Not true! Ants in the Northern Territory make great big ant mounds. These ant mounds provide new life. They are so strong in iron and calcium that they're better than anything humans can make to take when you're pregnant, if you have low iron, or anaemia. They are sterile. Ants go all over this country and they gather seeds, tiny seeds and they take them to their nests, remove and use the dangerous husks and leave the kernels. They're harvesters and threshers. Traditionally, we would go, scoop it all up and put it in a coolamon and winnow it. We then had our grain, some as tiny as poppy seeds that made gorgeous, gorgeous bread. We didn't kill anything, we took from the plant world mostly to survive; taking what we needed and not from greed. When you compare us to the ants in terms of their physical size in relation to the work they do, they are far more worthy. If we let go of our egos we'll realise this. So remember, in order to become part of the great Oneness we need to acknowledge the worthiness of all living beings. Then we can honour ourselves.

The spider! Nearly everybody hates spiders. They're creepy and they're crawly. But the spider is soooo good. When we become spiritually paralysed and we can't move, when we get all tangled and confused and we don't know Arthur from Martha, up from down, in from out, where do we go? Find a sitting place, call on the spirit of the spider because the spider makes the perfect web and the spider knows how to undo the web even after a storm. The spider is perfect at untangling webs and can show you how to rebuild. Your path is then clear again. So you have clarification, simply from a spider, another living being, whose light we need to survive. All light sources of Miwis are drawn to other light sources. Light attracts light.

Remember everything is a teaching. You get up in the morning, and out of the blue you see a parrot. It comes and lands right there. Ah, you're going on a journey. Then you're walking, and a white cockatoo swoops down. Ah, you're getting a message. The bees, the hardest workers, buzz-z-z-z around your favourite rose under your nose. Hullo, are you looking at yourself? What do you need to do about yourself as a unit in your family, your tribe or your community? It is the Oneness.

Chapter 4

SONGLINES

Every single thing has its essence and its essence is in the songlines. These are not to be confused with Dreaming tracks. Dreaming tracks manifest in the spiritual, songlines in the physical. Songlines are the essence of physical manifestations through Nungeena-tya. These essences continue to evolve as new species of plants, new emotions and changing of behaviour patterns. The essences in songlines are from Nungeena-tya, the earthly realms. There is even a human songline, the 'essence of' our strengths and weaknesses, our humanity. Songlines are the 'essence of' in honouring absolutely every single thing. Now this is what I mean about the Oneness — you must know enough about all things in your country and their purpose in order to honour them.

In our culture you're taught from the time you're tiny to see the songlines in the landscapes. You see them in the trees, the rocks, the ground, in the bush — everywhere. Depending where you are, you see koalas in everything, you see kangaroos in everything. Their very essence is imprinted in the land, every part of the land where their songlines go.

You've got to learn the essence of all of creation; you've got to lie and watch each animal and plant until you've got arthritis at fifteen! Just joking. You've got to know everything about them, even how you can mimic their language, their movement. That's why it's all done in the dance, so it's not forgotten and for you to understand the Oneness. So it means understanding everything about your country. It could seem really insignificant until you get right down into it, and then you think, 'That makes so much sense, that's why I've got to know everything.'

The songline that passes through your tribal land becomes your tribal totem/essence. I can tell within a few hundred metres when I'm moving from one tribal area to another. It's just so different; it's unbelievable how different it is. One part of me can't understand that people can't see this difference between one tribal land and another with different songlines. When you go on a trip, we're often not really in a good space but if you let go of all the garbage — like 'I've got to go there! I've got to get there because I'm thirsty. I've got to get this kid to the toilet' — you can't miss the songline signs. Everywhere you look you will see every tree is like a kangaroo. In another area everything is like a turtle, somewhere else everything is like a wombat, everything is like a serpent or everything is like a koala. The songlines leave their mark in the land. You just can't miss it, it's so absolutely there. But maybe I see it because in my early years that's all I saw.

Born on the Songlines

Every one of us has the essence of the songline that we were born to in our tribe. The major songline that passes on your land or through your tribal land becomes your tribal totem/essence. For your personal totem/essence it is where you were conceived that counts not where your parents bonded. So conceived isn't where they 'did the deed', it is where the mother was when the Spirit first entered her body, usually between the twelfth and sixteenth weeks of gestation. So it's when the mother feels the Spirit enter her body and move, this is when she is actually pregnant and the Spirit is there. Sometimes the elders sing a totem to a mother because they know her offspring will need the essence of a particular song. This is done once a woman is pregnant or they can sing the Spirit in and a pregnancy results.

Where a person is conceived and where a person is born makes a difference to the strengths and the essences that will come out. There was a little Koori girl born into a well-known tribe in 1975 who is the reincarnation of the Rainbow Serpent. This might happen only twice in 50 000 years but the old people have sung her up because they need the teachings for humanity. She will become well known worldwide by the time she is fifty — many, many will seek her out. She can be identified because the base of her skull is concave, because when the warriors were sent by Biami to slay the Rainbow Serpent they hit the serpent on the base of skull with a buundi (a club-like weapon).

If you know your children and you know their essence, you've got no worries. You say, 'OK, this is the turtle, I treat her like a turtle. This one

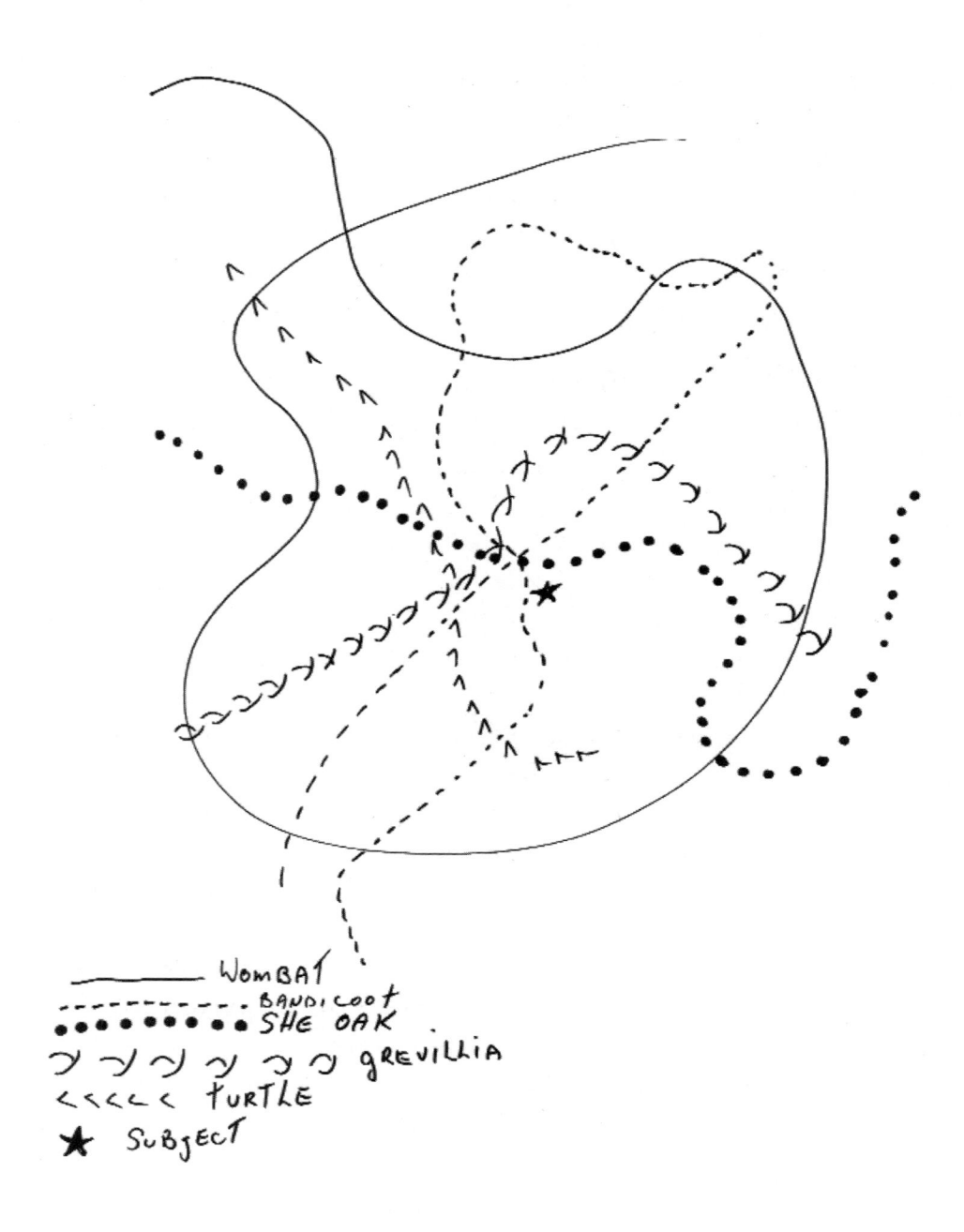

Illustration 4. *Songlines Map 1.*

is the she-oak; I treat her like the she-oak.' For knowing what your child is like, the major songlines are very important, especially the animal ones. If you look closely enough and you study the animals closely enough then you will recognise the child is the mirror essence of that part of Creation. Like colours emerging in a painting to make a whole picture, the old people can read the essences in the child even before the behaviour manifests. So they are always one jump ahead of them.

You've got to educate the children straightaway to understand their essences and what songlines are. Little kids are amazing in taking it in. Imagine if you were with me when you were about five or six and I'm sitting on the ground and I'm saying, 'Come here, lovely. Now this is you, you were born here. So you are the she-oak essence, so you can do this but you've got to be careful of your temper, you can have a very hot temper. So you need to think before you fire.'

Because children can let their essence take control, it is important for you to help them to continually learn to be in control. You tell them, say, about the bandicoot essence that they have. It starts from this age and you tell the stories over and over and over. So then your children know themselves so well they are on their way to becoming intimate with all their emotional characteristics. This is the lore/law. You must have an intimate relationship with all the emotions. Only then you'll know them so well and they'll be so familiar to you that they will never be able to control you. You will recognise when they begin to manifest; like a cold coming, they all have their symptoms.

There are conflicting essences that influence every single situation we encounter every day of our lives. This makes us human. Only if we have mastered our essences can we draw on the most appropriate response to each situation. This makes us strong and helps us walk our path. We have a responsibility to strengthen our children by helping them to understand and master their essences.

Songlines for Nienoj

To show where on the songlines a person is born I have drawn a map. The star on Songlines Map 1 (*Illustration 4*) marks where little Nienoj was born — exactly where he was born.

In this example there are the bandicoot, the she-oak, the honey grevillea, the turtle and the wombat songlines. Nienoj would be influenced by these five songline essences and thank god the influence of the wombat is a little bit further out.

Bandicoot

We'll deal with the bandicoot first because it is the closest songline and the most powerful influence for Nienoj. So we're talking about the spiritual essence now. We'll go right into the spiritual essence. The bandicoot is nocturnal, he can see in the night. That means the bandicoot has the capacity to see when all is darkest. Where other people get swamped and day turns into night and they can't bear it anymore, the bandicoot sees in the night. By having his nocturnal vision, he has an amazing capacity to find solutions to problems others would find difficult to solve, for example problems of family and community breakdown because of emotional upheaval. Bandicoots can be highly skilled in developing strategies for defending our country if it comes under threat. When times are darkest for everyone else, lo and behold the bandicoots, who you have often wanted to murder because they are constant trouble makers, come into their positive power — Mister or Missus solution in the flesh!

The bandicoot can also be very destructive. He can be seen as a troublemaker if he is not educated in his essence. Because he sees and digs in the dark a bandicoot cannot be trusted while young, or maybe never, with a secret; chances are he will spill his guts quicker than if you gave him a bottle of Ipecac syrup. Bandicoots have this habit of looking for secrets; they are good at digging in dirt. Bandicoots often turn out to be reporters, media people, spies and politicians. They dig and dig and dig. If you have a songline crossing itself where it influences a person you have double the effect so in this case, unless little Nienoj is instructed from early childhood to acknowledge and recognise his self-essence, you will have a person shunned by society, because nobody will stand him if his ruling essence runs out of control, unchecked — you'll have a real poison, a nasty on your hands. You do not want this for your child, if you see it emerging you have a responsibility to say to your child, 'You are mastered by the bandicoot, channel your nocturnal vision into becoming a scientific researcher or a forensic scientist, a private investigator or at worst an industrial spy.' There is always, and I stress this, there is always a positive way to manifest your most negative essence. It just takes acceptance and guidance by the Elders and yourself.

Little Nienoj has absorbed some of the essence of the bandicoot. You all know someone who is the biggest shit-stirrer you've ever met in your life. But when things get really tough this terrible shit-stirrer, who you want to spend your life strangling, comes to the fore and says, 'No, no we need to do this, this and this.' And you go, 'Just when I wanted you dead, you blossom.' The bandicoot has the ability to find a solution to a problem, even when everyone else gives up. Often he can see a big problem emerging within the family unit long before anyone else. When a bandicoot speaks out about it people often become angry and refer to him as a doomsayer or drama queen. Then they won't admit it when the bandicoot is proved to be right. It's the essence of the bandicoot; he can be very destructive because when he digs a bandicoot tends to get inside you and churn up all that stuff that we really don't want to look at. He does it within families; he is the family shit-stirrer.

But where the bandicoot digs at night, that's where the very fragile seeds drop and the water fills up in that little hole and the seed is given a chance to grow. So they have a very positive aspect, when you dig things up and open them out. It's like when you turn the compost heap. What happens? Things grow. So we're looking at the essence of the bandicoot completely.

She-oak

The next closest songline essence to Nienoj is she-oak. The influence of this essence would make Nienoj easy to befriend, marry, work or parent with. Whenever you see she-oaks near the beach then there is sacred water, so they are life givers. Because they have the essence of sacred water four days after their nuts have dropped they can be gathered and used to stop dehydration. The nuts have absorbed endurance. If the nut has been dry for a few days and you're walking through the desert and you bite on that every so often, don't chew it all up, it releases a sap that reduces the body's dehydration rate by up to 90%. You can actually conserve your moisture, and thus conserve your energy.

So the she-oak has incredible endurance. If Nienoj is influenced by the she-oak, he really has some staying power, and can go and go and go. He can take a real lot before being knocked down. And since she-oak wood can be split very easily to make roofs, it also has an element of protection. These are its strengths. The she-oak's weakness, however, is that when it burns it makes one of the hottest fires. This influence is a hot, hot fiery temper — a real fiery temper that can get Nienoj into trouble. This is not like the influence of spinifex. If you are born along this songline there is a little grass fire. Poof! Real hot! There's a flare-up, scorching someone's butt and then it dies straight out — and the person makes you a cup of tea! With the she-oak, the embers linger so they fester. With this influence Nienoj can be in danger of doing physical and emotional harm to others. Many people, who have committed crimes of passion or rage murders, have probably been influenced by a she-oak in their essences.

Honey Grevillea

Then we come to the honey grevillea, a weaker influence on Nienoj. Honey grevilleas provide sustenance, they give food. So the honey grevillea's influence will be a nurturing one. He could be someone that you can leave the little ones with — but don't be a bit surprised if you come home and find the little ones with a big slap around the ears. They will be nurtured, protected and chastised. The negative of the grevillea's influence is Nienoj could allow himself to be drained by giving too much. It's a nectar tree, so it draws the birds. It draws and draws to itself those seeking nourishment. Those who have grevillea as a major essence are people who are likely to give, give, give and then one day go, 'I'm sick of this.' They have a problem in recognising when enough is enough.

So the grevillea gives life and nurtures; it also provides shade and protection. Grevilleas grow in masses, mini forests, and are thick, making them the ideal place for small birds to nest and survive. They can sustain weaker creatures. They also build very good ground cover from their seedpods and leaf matter, again providing for other life forms. Grevilleas will always attract life and be popular. They should always be planted in clumps, as they like being with each other.

Australia's native plants contain some of the highest levels of cyanide and alkaloid in the world. This also influences Nienoj. The essence appears as beautiful and strong but there is underlying poison. You must also remember everything has a negative side, absolutely everything. It started at the very moment of Creation. Many native plants have levels of toxins — some are mild, but some are deadly poison. The levels of toxins can also vary greatly in the life cycle of the plant. This is very important to remember. See what I mean about getting to know your country and every single thing in it! Then you'll know when to harvest or how to heat one with another to kill the poison. That way you'll survive.

Turtle

Now we are moving outward to weaker influences. This does not mean the turtle is a weaker essence, it means its influence is less. The positive of the turtle is that he carries everything he needs on his back, including his house, so he doesn't have to rely on anybody else. The essence of the turtle is autonomy. If Nienoj stays overnight he doesn't have to put up with all that 'of course you can stay' shit, because he can be with others yet apart from them. What you could find yourself saying to these people is 'Will you please get out of the toilet?' or 'Haven't you eaten your cereal yet?' Doesn't matter how much you whip a turtle it will just go into its shell.

The turtle is not fast but he is very focused on his path. So Nienoj would be someone who depends very little on other people for emotional or spiritual support. He would be spiritually contained and focused and often called a loner or aloof. Turtles' shells are protective, they are not as thin-skinned as other creatures and when they have had enough they can instantly withdraw into their own space. Turtles are excellent at meditation, long-term isolated retreats and are not whingers. You have a turtle if your child always wants to dress herself, feed herself from when she is a tiny baby, is not very responsive to your cuddles (there is nothing wrong with your cuddles) and doesn't want you to tie her shoe laces up; it means you've got an independent child. If you think from the moment that child could walk, 'Gosh, she's so independent,' you know you've got a turtle on your hands.

Turtles are very sensitive and trauma, usually to their Miwis, from events like the death of loved ones, separation or betrayal, all of which flip turtles on their backs. They become spiritually paralysed, and can die or commit suicide. They have vulnerable areas at points around their shells and when turtles do go on their backs you have to spend a lot of energy turning them over. You have to turn them over spiritually, emotionally and mentally or they may never recover because their Miwis can die. Quite often I've seen people who are turtles spend their lives in mental institutions because no one seems to have understood that they're turtles and it is not known how to help people with turtle essence. You can't walk up to a turtle on his back and go, 'Hey, you get up! Go on, get up! Wake up to yourself! Get a life!' All a turtle will do is spin and spin around — and that's the truth of it.

Wombat

The last songline on Nienoj's map is the wombat. Wombats are stubborn and only see what they want to see. They're short-sighted, indeed nearly blind. I'm giving you the negative of the wombat first. So quite often with you stubborn people it's not that you can't see, but that you don't want to see. You don't want to see the other side of things. It's like too much wombat. 'No, no, no, no, no. I don't want to see it.' So you make yourself moogeenge and that's the thing about the wombat.

But the wombat has a very good side. If you live on a wombat songline or you have wombats around your property or home, you will be blessed with incredible strength, endurance and determination from the essence of the wombat. This creature is blessed with one of the highest levels of integrity. It doesn't want to take over anyone else's territory; it just wants to be left alone. It has no spite essence. To kill a wombat is to bring the wrathful essence of wombat upon you — very bad luck. So don't build your house, dam or shed on a wombat trail.

In this world today we very much need the strength and protection of the wombat essence. To prove this, search around for people who have left wombats to live in peace on their land and notice their good fortune against the bad luck of those who have destroyed wombats and their habitat. Check the prices they get for their cattle on sale days. The wombat is one of the most determined creatures. And by golly, if the wombat wants something, the wombat gets something. The wombat doesn't care if it's got to go straight through a mountain. It doesn't care if it's got to go under a dam and drown itself. It will get there. That's what a wombat does. 'You won't beat me. You won't beat me.' Often you beat yourself because you have too much determination, and an obsessive personality. What's the use in drowning just to make a point?

Songlines for Esme

Let's say your birthplace is the star on Songlines Map 2 (*Illustration 5*) and your name is Esme. You are about the same distance from the wombat and bandicoot songlines and they are your strongest influences. (Refer to 'Songlines for Nienoj' on pages 46–51 for descriptions of these influences.)

Tribal

The dotted line on the map is the wombat but in this example it is also your tribal songline. In each of the other two examples there would also be a tribal songline. To this line you now have a lifelong responsibility to sing up, honour, pray and do ceremony. You will not eat this animal, kill this animal or injure this animal in any way. This animal is now as important to you as your kin. If this animal is injured even today, your first priority is to see to its suffering and if possible its survival. I don't care if you are in a hurry to get to some meeting, work or play. STOP! You cannot go past without assisting your totem. You have a Spirit commitment to ensure this species' survival continues.

A totem/essence has also been sung to you by the old people; this is a secondary influence to your tribal totem/essence. In this example

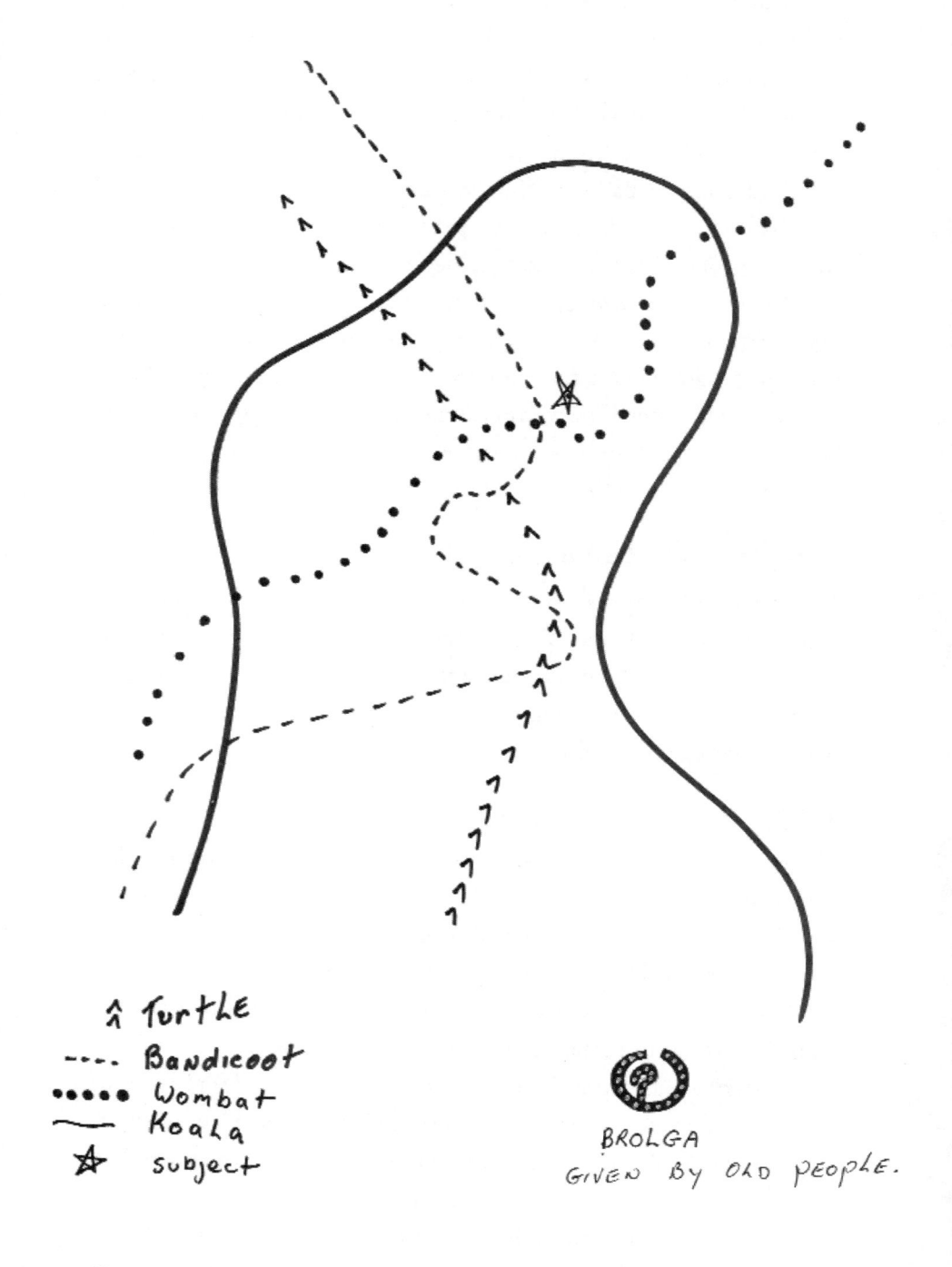

Illustration 5. Songlines Map 2.

your sung essence is brolga to make you more complex. Now you cannot kill the brolga either. The other totemic influences that are further afield you will still honour but hunting them becomes your choice. We see our tribal totemic influences as being as sacred to us as life itself. Traditionally the honouring of the tribal totem is strict and it is policed well. Who will you make the most effort for — your family or your neighbour? These totems are now your kin and you will be influenced for life from these essences.

The influence of turtle is still close enough to have a major effect. You won't quite be a loner but you will need a place to retreat to even if it is just in your mind. Perhaps your partner will often say, 'I speak to you but you don't seem to be here. You are off in your shell somewhere. (Refer to 'Songlines for Nienoj' on pages 49–50 for more information.)

Koala

I have also put the koala on this map because it is a native animal with its own teaching. Laziness and slothfulness — that is the negative side of koala. Koalas will always be looking for short cuts when asked to do a task — one nail instead of two; wipe one side of the plate when washing up and forget the cutlery, just pile it all into a tea towel and shake; they never want to do their homework, never. True koalas usually become beach bums, naturalists or dope smokers. Koalas can spend their entire lives up a tree stoned.

The positive side of the koala is that they have very little greed in essence and you will find the koala will always wait until last even if they miss out. They have genuine calmness. This is good for you because you also have the influence of the brolga.

Brolga

This powerful influence lends more to greed: 'What I see, I want. If someone else has it, I must too, at any cost.' For someone who is married to a brolga, it is tough. You will always be in debt and have half a million bloody credit cards all maxed out. In fairness to the brolga they have a very generous side as well, sometimes too generous. They are usually graceful, but most kleptomaniacs are true brolgas. What I mean by true

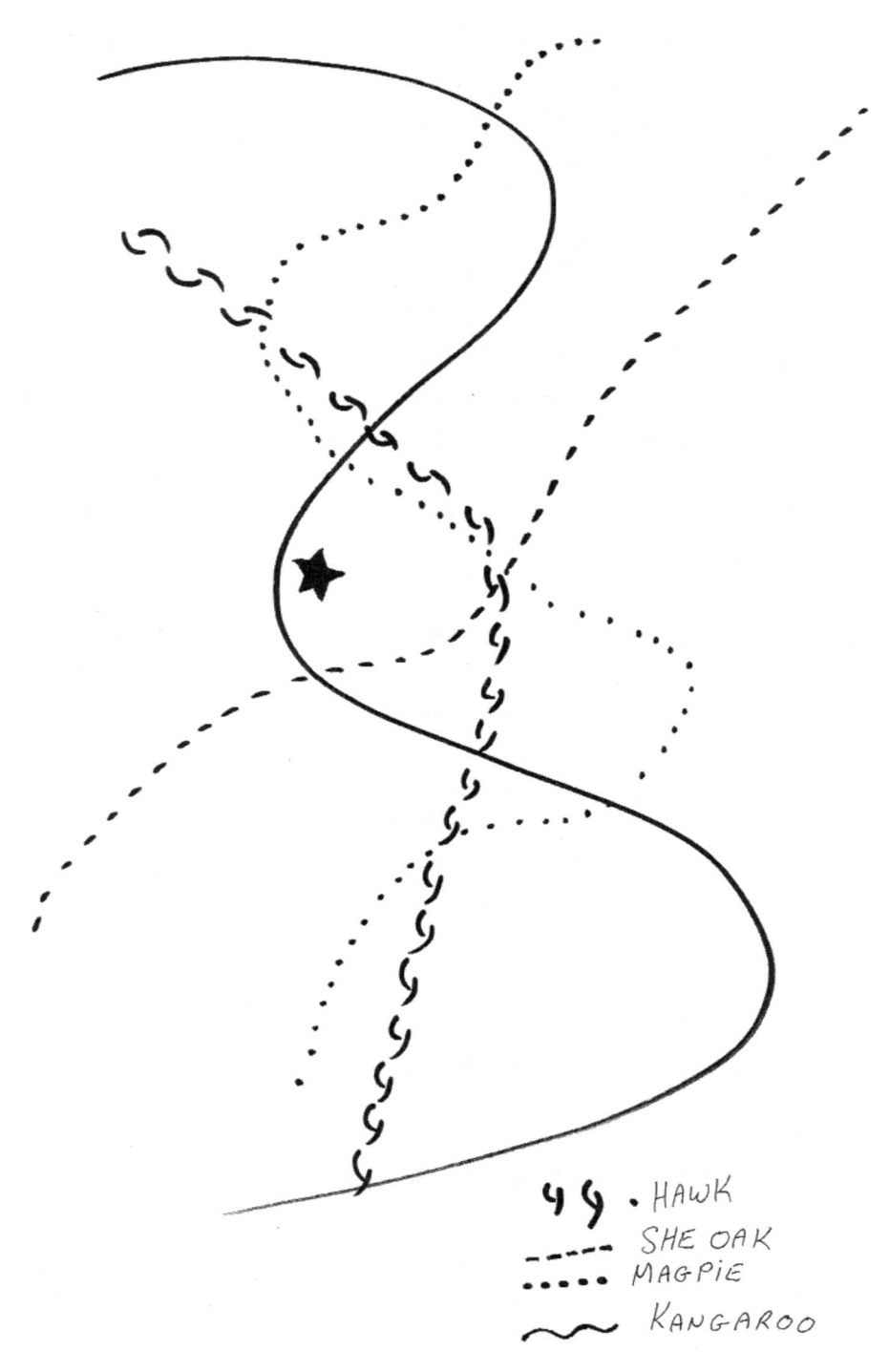

Illustration 6. *Songlines Map 3.*

is this totem's essence is the major influence on this person's life. It is OK to be what you are — but the greatest teaching is getting to really understand your weaknesses and strengths without judgment. The teaching says, 'We are perfectly imperfect. Knowing your true essence and managing it means you will fulfil your life's journey.'

Songlines for Kara

Let's consider another example. I'll call this person Kara. Look at Songlines Map 3 (*Illustration 6*). Kara was born here very close to the kangaroo songline. The human essence of Kara will be strongly influenced by this songline. You know how some people get into living in the past; they are under the influence of the yabby songline or totem. 'This has happened to me, that has happened; suffering ... suffering ... suffering, in the past ... in the past ... in the past. When I was young the world was a better place, less crime, people cared about each other etc.' Or, 'I don't like these tomatoes, they were much better last season.' They always want to go back to yesterday or feel that living in the past is far better than living in the present.

Kangaroo

A kangaroo, however, can't go into the past. Because of what happened with Biami,[8] she can only go forward. It's the only animal that can just go forward, she can't go backwards. You can call on the essence of the kangaroo to take you forward. So Kara with her kangaroo essence is a person who goes, 'Oh, don't talk to me about the past.' So if you get someone in your family who goes, 'Oh, for God's sake, will you think about tomorrow, the future, instead of, like, what happened to you, like 25,000 million years ago?' you can guarantee that person is influenced by the kangaroo, and she understands she is kangaroo essence. You can't fight them and say, 'Well, you've got no compassion.' Yet that's what we do, we say, 'Well, you know, you mongrel! I want you to listen to my suffering.' But she has the essence of kangaroo, so she needs to move forward and she'll try to pull people forward with her. Kangaroos are leaders. They will cheer things up and take people out of their self-imposed shit. All this will be a major influence on Kara.

under the quandong tree

Now let's look at the weaknesses of the kangaroo. If the kangaroo has broken her tail she loses her balance and is buggered. She needs to know that there's only so much that she can take. If she's deeply injured spiritually there's a chance of her becoming immobile. If she experiences trauma, death or betrayal — a kangaroo isn't good with betrayal — she can fade away. If the spirit is too damaged she may give up on life completely.

Kangaroos are very dignified, even when dying. They wait for death to arrive and go peacefully and calmly. We injure many kangaroos on the roads and leave them to die but sometimes, even with no water to drink, this can take nine days. If you hit a kangaroo you are spiritually obligated to end their suffering. Cowardice is one of our most terrible opponents. The more we run from our spiritual responsibility, the more the shadow of cowardice engulfs us. If we try to convince ourselves that the animal will die within an hour or two of shock we are deluded. If you don't have a tool, use a big stick or rock to knock it on the back of the head and end its suffering. Cover its head first, even if you have to use your own T-shirt. This can be an act of courage and compassion on your part and fulfils your spiritual obligation. At the end of your life the suffering you have inflicted on another creature is your responsibility — your karma. Understanding the essences of your songlines takes ages. You've got to observe the kangaroo and everything she does. You've got to know her so intimately, and that goes on for your lifetime. We have to understand ourselves, and then we can understand others.

Magpie

So if you look again at Songlines Map 3 (*Illustration 6*) you will see that, in this example of Kara, after the kangaroo the next biggest songline influence would be the she-oak. This has a similar influence for Kara as it did for Nienoj in our first example. A lesser influence for Kara would be the magpie. I'm a magpie and I talk to myself. I talk to myself all the time — and I answer. I walk around by myself and I say, 'You bloody thing, you won't even straighten out.' Magpies are notorious for giving themselves a bad time. I don't know what I'm going to do with myself, so I talk to myself and never shut up! That's a magpie trait. Her weakness is she probably talks too much until her throat is sore.

A magpie is extremely territorial. If she's threatened she'll get vicious. A magpie will caw, 'What are you doing in my room? Get him out of my room!' or 'That's my part of my yard. Git! Don't touch my ball. Give me back my disk.' She is absolutely territorial, and if you're her parent you think, 'Oh shit, I've got a magpie. That's the last thing I need.' But once you know it, you understand it, and it's OK with a magpie. When she's out of control, you know she is being territorial, so you give her a little bit and then send her packing to her own little space — her room.

A magpie child is one of the easiest to identify and understand because she is so in your face with her essence. Thankfully she will become a strong and hard-working adult with the ability to support her family, including her siblings, through almost anything. Never let her rule when young, because magpies will. She'll say, 'Get out of my bathroom. Get out of my toilet. Get out of my yard.' You'll know when she is going to be vicious. So what you've got to do with a magpie, from the time she's two or three, is give her a little bit of her own territory. 'This is your little space, only this, OK?' So then she feels validated and she's fine. So that's what you do with a magpie.

The magpie's strength is her loyalty and commitment to family/clan. She can be so loyal it leads her into danger even for family or friends. A magpie needs to be careful her loyalty is not taken for granted or abused. A magpie usually helps her parents raise the younger siblings before she goes off and mates, unlike most other birds who stay within their clan but leave the family once they leave the nest.

Another important trait of magpie essence that needs to be understood is that she will feed her young right into adulthood, much longer than many other birds. As a personal example, I have a forty-two year old that I still try to baby. The bottom line for a magpie is she keeps to her own. Humans with magpie essence are often fanatics and racists. However, with good self-understanding, magpies are strong enough to protect the weak and vulnerable and will be totally committed once they have chosen their life's path.

Hawk

Then there's the influence of the hawk essence on Kara. The hawk is a visionary because it can see so well. The child that's born on the hawk songline, or has the hawk essence, always pre-empts the situation. She already knows she's in the shit, before you even say, 'You're grounded.' Even as you say the word 'grounded', she'll be on her way to her room. So this Kara pre-empts most things; she really knows you and the family, probably better than any of the others. She'll have real foresight too and she can speak about 'down the track,' especially once she's adult. She could say, 'This may be a mistake because down the track maybe this could happen or that could happen.' She is very sharp at it.

The hawk is also a bird of prey. The hawk's weakness is that she's capable of feeding off weaker prey. If she has a brother or a sister that's a turtle, she can really take advantage.

The Essence of that Contained

Traditionally Koori kids are educated in their songlines: 'This is your strength and this is your weakness. This is who you are and you must know yourself, so that you don't let the negative parts of you take over or you become bugeenge.' Yes, fear is used but it's like the child thinks, 'Gee! I don't want to turn into that permanently, forever!'

So there's a songline of everything and a songline is 'the essence of that contained' from Nungeena-tya. The separate essence of what was created. We're all influenced by songlines. There might be 300 separate bits and pieces of information with the essences of the songlines that make up an individual. There are major songlines and tribal songlines.

My songline is a warrigul, which is the dingo, that's my tribal songline. My job is to forever protect and sing up the songline of the dingo, to ensure the continuance of its species. I can't eat dingo. I must protect it at all times, because it is my tribal totem. And my personal totem, as I've said, is the magpie, better known as billinga. Being born on the warrigul songline means I have endurance, stealth, knowing and very keen senses. Now for the negative side — we hunt in packs and, when cornered, are very savage. I'm aware of that.

If you could go to a school and say, 'OK, I'll draw a map of everything that I am aware of about me, all my positive and negative attributes', how differently would you see life? More importantly, how differently would you live your life, how differently would you respond to others around you, and their essences and all the creatures of Creation? Would you respond to their weaknesses with your weaknesses or your strengths? How would you then raise your children if you started to become aware of their true essences as they grew? Would you approach child-raising differently? Would you teach your children the importance of being boss of self? Would you allow enough scope and guidance to encourage them to understand their own essences, negative and positive, and teach them how to maintain those essences in a spiritually, physically and mentally healthy way? Hopefully 'yes', but probably 'no' because it is likely our egos would prevent us. If you encourage your child to be boss of self, this truly means boss of self. It would mean not stuffing your religious beliefs down your child's throat, not choosing their friends, not demanding they become doctors, lawyers, politicians, clerics and so forth. We often try to fulfil the failed dreams of our own lives through our children because our parents stole our dreams from us so now we take our turn to become the thieves.

Songlines are very, very important. Every single tribal group on this planet is responsible for a songline. They may not call them songlines, but they are responsible. Some groups say emblems or mascots. They are referring to something they've always got but they can use all different words for it.

You can walk along the songline. The dingo songline goes right around the Earth. It starts being called a warrigul songline and goes up through my country, through Parkingee around through Arrernte, up through the middle of Uluru and then up and over the water and to another country where it is called the wolf songline, and then it goes on to be called something else. It is the dog songline and it goes right around the Earth.

Other songlines also continue right around the planet. In different parts of the world there will be animals with the same essences, they will just look different. For example, I'm sure there is another animal that represents laziness and apathy like the koala. Certain creatures are unique to Australia so their songlines are only to be found here, like the kangaroo. Remember the Creator said these animals will live in harmony with the keepers of Creation. They do not hunt humans like other padded footed animals. There are other creatures around the Earth given by Biami, from the Rivers of the Dreaming, as a reward to a nation or individual for keeping His lore/law. From that day forward (the day of the gifting) the people would benefit, forever. For example there is a North American Indian teaching about the killer whale and the osprey and their unconditional love for each other. The teaching is similar to the platypus teaching in our tradition and their union was similarly blessed by Biami.[9]

There are human songlines too, but — as I found out purely by accident — the strongest of these is in India. I think it goes from India over into Pakistan. Probably that's why the spirituality colours[10] are so extreme in spite of the poverty and everything else in India. The colours are the most amazing I've ever seen in my entire life. When you are on a songline the essences are magnified. It seems that in India they understand on a higher level the briefness of the human journey of each life. The further away we are from the human songline perhaps we get into fear more. In their colours there is little fear essence.

A human songline carries the traits of humans, the essence of humans, who we are. It's like a carrot tastes like a carrot, it carries the essence of a carrot. It's just the essence of humans — all that makes us up — the vulnerabilities and the fears, every single aspect, our positives and our negatives. The same as anything else, we're not separate from anything else. We are no better, no different, and no more important — believe you me — than, say, even the trees. As we kill them, as we chop them down and their lives die away, so do ours. They make the oxygen that we so desperately need for life, to sustain ourselves. People go out and bulldoze down trees. They say, 'I need to clear my paddocks.' They clear, clear, clear ... for the view! They say, 'I'll go and poison that tree there, because I can't see the harbour view!' What happens when they're out in the burning sun, and their brains are getting fried? Who do they turn to? The poor old tree. It's a case of 'hug me now, protect me now'. These are the things we need to be aware of and think deeply about.

Singing Up

Songlines are the essence of all that has been created. For example, in Creation Dreaming time, during the last week in September and the first two weeks in October, everyone has a role in singing up their totem. Your tribal totem and your personal totem — this is your responsibility. You can't eat your tribal totem and you can't kill it. So if everyone reading this book took up responsibility for a different personal totem and a tribal totem, we would have started ensuring that nothing becomes extinct. You are as responsible for that totem as you are for your own safety and you sing it up and you honour it up.

Singing up is similar, for example, to say me being a Catholic and wanting to sing up peace in the world. I would be saying, 'Hail Mary, full of grace' and I'd do all of those and I'd do so many 'Our Fathers' and I would do a lot more of the rosary too. For Anglicans it would be prayers and hymns. If I was a Buddhist and I was wanting to sing up peace and healing, I would meditate, do mantras. If I was Hindu I would do puja and kirtin. Singing up is a form of praying. Singing, like those in Israel at the Wailing Wall singing their prayers. You sing up the songlines because of your totem's essence; the essence of the songline becomes your totem.

So the singing up Kooris have done is like a lot of praying. They do it with dance and singing; singing up is praying and honouring. There are many ceremonies that go on and on, singing up the songlines. I've said before everything has to be validated in order to continue to grow and multiply. This is so important; this is your task, your responsibility to your tribal songline. For example, if you are a Koori or you know these teachings this is what I would expect of you under the lore/law. Suppose you are driving from Sydney to Canberra for a very important two-legged meeting. You are running late because one of your kids is very sick — and lying on the side of the road is your totem, injured. Your first Miwi responsibility, under the lore/law, is to your totem — that's your essence. Don't you dare pass the bloody buck onto WIRES, the National Park Rangers, the Department of Wildlife or anybody else. This is your essence, this sustains your life.

You've probably heard the term: 'Oh, that one's been sung!' There is another level of all this, but it doesn't occur often, a way of singing or praying for the bad things to happen. It's not good.

The important thing is to sing up the songlines so they don't become extinct. What happened to the fairies? People stopped singing them up. What happened to the dinosaurs? Probably people stopped singing them up. If you take a baby, and put the baby in a cot and feed her and feed her and feed her but do not nurture her or nurse her — in other words, you do not sing her up — you can feed her all you like and she will still waste away. She will fail to thrive.

Finding Your Songlines

Suppose you want to find out what songlines you or your children were born on. Where do you start?

- Firstly, look at a traditional map of Australia and find out what tribe you belong to. What is your tribal country? It has nothing to do with your colour; it has to do with your country.

I'll give you a couple of examples. If you were born somewhere from Dunedoo to the Blue Mountains to Lake Cargelligo to Albury, then within this area you are Wirradjirri. The main songline going through Wirradjirri is warrigul; there are many others but the tribal totem for Wirradjirri is warrigul. If you are born in Eora land you are of the dolphin tribe, so water will have a great influence. Up near Lismore and back down through Alstonville just around Byron Bay there's the turtle songline and that's where they're all 'happy' people. They're really laid back and nobody hurries. They might say, 'What's the rush? This is cool! Just have another smoke' because it's a turtle songline, their essence. When it's the honey bee songline, the essence changes. From Wilcannia to Broken Hill down in a curve and then back across to Bourke is the eagle songline. It is the only place in Australia where the hawk songline doubles back and crosses over the eagle songline; by something doubling back over itself its influence is compounded. This makes it a very powerful place. When it's full of shit, it's full of shit! Up that area, as you know, it is usually full of shit, because they're digging and digging the mines, they're damaging Nungeena-tya. There's often a lot of sad sorrow and grieving in Wilcannia.

- Secondly, I would go to the local Land Council or Koori community and ask to talk to some of the old elders. Just go along and ask, 'What's the totem of this tribe and what other songlines are in your country?' Someone will know. A lot of old people now are coming out and telling the stories. Every tribe has got its tribal totem. They all know that, even though our society has fallen apart and become fractured. A lot of them have chosen to become Christians or go another way of spiritual belief; they still all know their tribal totems and their country's songlines. The elders know which songlines cross.

- Thirdly, observe your child and yourself and really get to know the native plants and animals of our countries. I can't stress this enough and I can't do it for you.

I could write a book on Songlines but you'd need a truck to carry it around. If I really went into doing the essences of one single person, I would need to include the essences of all that grows in the area which could be 3000 plants, the river and the essences it brings, and the major animal songlines. Then I'd need to break down all that grows there into smaller parts, for example, medicine bushes like the quinine songline. (Quinine is a powerful medicine bush that is used to treat kidney and liver diseases.) Yathandah (emu bush) are also powerful medicine bushes. There could be old man weed, and even the slipper orchid. Do you know how delicate and sensitive the slipper orchid is? But what an amazing survivor! It will wither at the top and there will be nothing, no sign of it to the naked eye. Because I can see its colours I can find it. Underneath the ground it is still absolutely complete, strong and full. So it's one of those with the hidden strength and the hidden endurance.

All this takes a lifetime to learn. I've been at it for five decades and still I know so little, just a tiny little bit. It would take me a long time to find it all out but I could write a book. It would need to take so much into account. I would have to get the exact map of the Earth and as I moved out of my tribal area, I'd need to confer with the mob next door and next door again and so on. Then it would become the effort of all the older women to put it together. It would take such a long, long time.

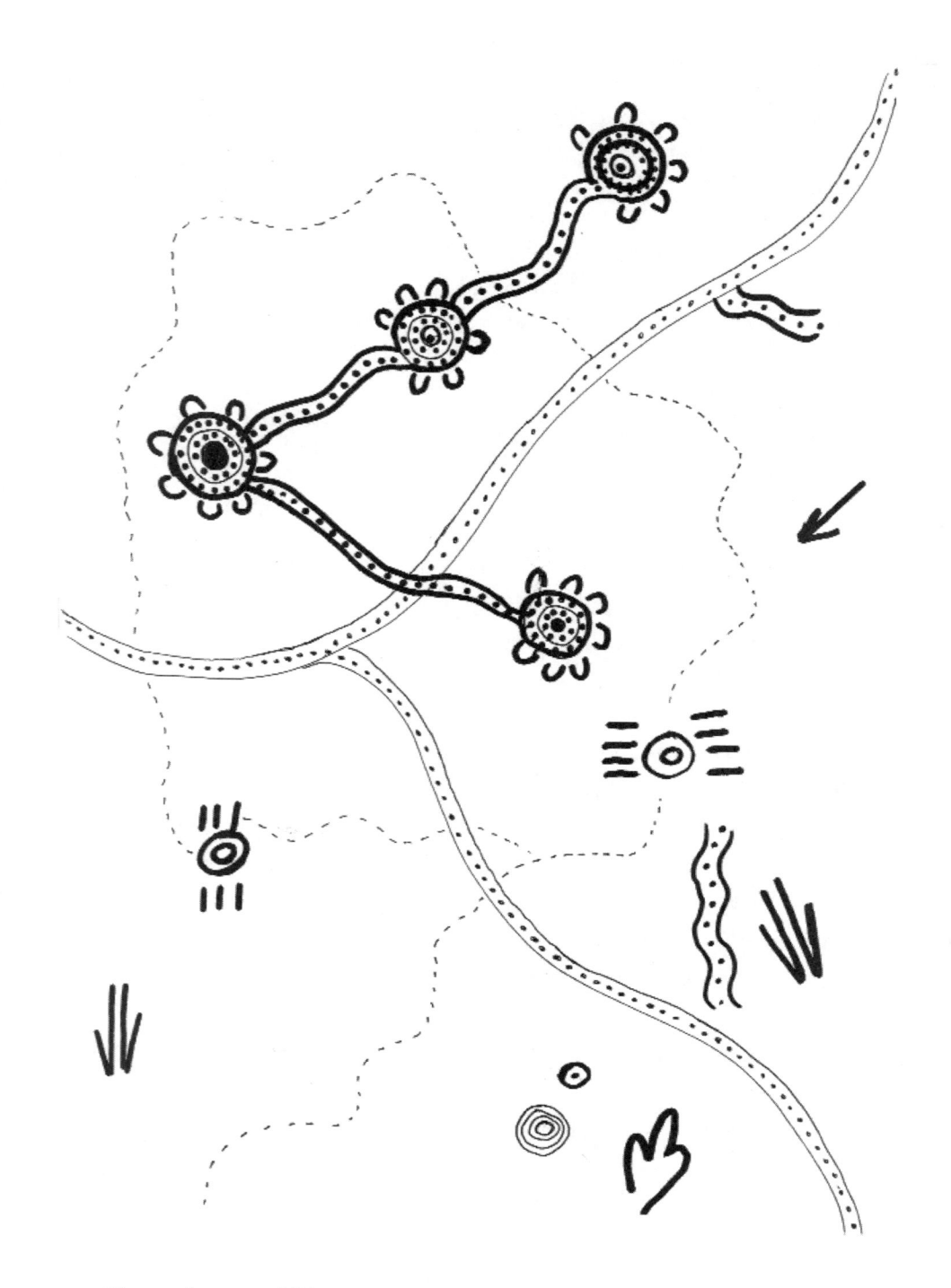

Illustration 7. *A Child's Dreaming Story.*

My wish is that every single child that starts school in this country, by the time they finish kindergarten, would be able to do their own Dreaming story, according to tradition. They should have old people, like me, coming in and showing them a map (for instance like that in *Illustration 7*) and saying to them, 'This Dreaming track means this, and this songline means that, and this songline is this essence. You see, this is a story about a country, about a mother and a father and a family and their journey, traveling around their tribal area, over the kangaroo songline, hunting kangaroos, chasing emu eggs along the grasslands, going to rivers and waterfalls where it rains a lot, and hitting the desert where there are more emus.'

It's all about knowing where you belong. It's OK to be, say, an Anglican Christian child being reared in Australia and getting the Anglican teachings but still learning how to do your own Dreaming story in school. And it's all right for a child to be brought up in Australia in the Muslim faith and learn to do this in school. It's about our country and identity and it's all right to be different. So if they learn, while we're still alive, about songlines and singing them up it could become similar to praying for good things to happen. We do it in song.

I had a garden once, up on a mountain and I put in all these unwanted lasiandras and sang. This garden was there for only four to five years but it looked like it had been there for twenty or more, because I just sang it up. What you do is you go along your songlines, singing them up. You sing up people too, but the only singing non-Koori people have heard of makes them go, 'Oooh, if they sing you up, something terrible is going to happen to you.' It's not like that at all. It's good singing, it's powerful singing, it's honouring the land. If you honour the land you honour the Creator who created the land. You give thanks for what you have. That's what's important! Very important!

I can only give you permission to take up what is rightfully yours and that is your sense of belongingness to this, our country. By giving permission for the belongingness to our country I'm beginning to sing the songlines for you, wherever you are. It is up to you then to keep them alive.

Chapter 5

MIWI

The teachings and stories about Creation, Dreaming, Dreaming tracks and songlines need to be repeated over and over and over. If you don't know these nothing else flows. You must always know where your journey starts and we must never, ever forget who created us and who nurtures us every single day of our existence. I never get sick of telling about these things because they just encapsulate the essence of all.

I have no explanation of why the Rainbow Serpent was born as two joined together and therefore what we inherited. Life after life our struggle is to keep anger and compassion in balance and not to keep trying to delete one or the other. When we do have these emotions in balance we are connected more strongly to the Oneness. So we each choose the teachings, one or two, to learn in this life's journey, those that will bring us closer to this balance.

Everything in Creation has its own teaching story. Different stories can hold the same teaching, so the vehicle can change. Even if we are in the same tradition we don't all hear the same message or see the same view. On our spiritual journey we can have a different interpretation of the same teaching, depending on where we are with struggling and yearning. There is no right or wrong interpretation of the teachings — only whether, at any moment in time, they give us what we need to take the next step on our path.

Your Miwi is not the same age as your body. It's probably thousands of years old — it has wisdom and can guide you. A good teacher can use words in a singing up way, aiming directly at the Miwi and pulling the Miwi out from its sleep and shutting down the conscious mind. To stimulate the memory of how you used to be before the Miwi shut down, you must stimulate all your senses — sight, sound, touch and smell. When I see people who are suffering, I trigger them by saying something or stopping and telling a story that will help them understand themselves. Sometimes we are so filled with sadness, worry or grief we can't step outside ourselves and look back in because we are so deep in one of these feelings. We know that it is often someone there at the time who stops us and says what they can see happening.

The traditional way is to be told a story that applies to our situation. We are always better at holding stories and it helps us save face. Think of a time in your life when a significant event has happened — like a baby's birth, a parent's death, or a marriage — and think of the song you heard on the day of that event. For your whole life you will never forget that song. It's the same when you hear a story or wise talk that helps you understand and feel better. Then you become a teacher and you tell the story or talk the wise talk to someone else in a similar situation. If you teach properly and go for the Miwi it can be as if the listeners have been asleep for hundreds of years and are waking up. Sometimes I see people fifteen years later and they say, 'My life is so, so different and it started at that weekend you taught us.' You see incredible changes that can even surprise me.

Awakening Your Miwi

The first step to awakening your Miwi is to give permission to forgive yourself for your mistakes and to realise you are human and so perfectly imperfect. Emotions like guilt and shame build such a wall around your Miwi that it is almost snuffed out by the energy boulders of these emotions; then mind and ego rules. A long time ago I remember Agi, a teacher, telling me things and I asked her, 'Will this make me good at what I do?' She answered, 'You are only what YOU strive to be.' I took this literally that I could strive to be the best wife, mother, worker in the world. It wasn't until I was about twenty-seven that I realised I just wanted to be more compassionate and tolerant and less judgmental. This has been one of my greatest realisations in all aspects of my journey because with less judging, and more compassion and tolerance, I would be a better grain of sand in the Oneness of Creation.

If you listen to your Miwi with integrity you can't go wrong. Your journey will be on the path that you chose when you incarnated. It's your knowing. When we are born we know everything, then between three and five years old, a veil descends over our memories. Between five and puberty, under the lore/law, children have no gender responsibility. They are simply allowed to unfold and be a child. Spatters of stories are told, encouraging them to listen to their Miwis or to trust self. 'You're born boss of self' is drummed into these children. This is very good because, unlike the Western way, these children learn very quickly — but in a safe way and at a very young age — about action and consequence. Right on the periphery there is always a granny or elder keeping a close eye so they are not harmed.

That's what we have to stay with. Our Miwi is saying, 'Yes, yes. No, no. Go here.' Sometimes the Universe will do everything to block us. Things will just hammer you and hammer you, until you wake up one day and think, 'OK, yeah, I get it, I know I'm not supposed to be doing this, and I'm supposed to be doing that. OK, I get it.'

We need to understand that if we make every decision, from this day on, with our Miwis we'll never make another mistake. Truly, we will not make another mistake on our spiritual journey. So I say to everyone — even my own children — listen to your Miwis. If we don't we can find ourselves in situations that are really, really bad and years later we'll realise that we've made terrible, terrible mistakes. Remember, let every mistake be your own because from that comes the greatest teaching and if you really learn from a mistake you never make it again. Often you're told 'You should do this, you must do that'. We are worn down and down and down until we ignore our Miwis although we know we shouldn't. It's easier, it makes for less conflict, especially with people who do have a big influence in our lives — parents, siblings, peers and friends. We are so vulnerable because we've been conditioned and we don't have any confidence in self. Even if a teacher that you have followed for years instructs you to do a task and your Miwi goes, 'No this is wrong' then you need to follow your Miwi and not your teacher. At the end of the day you alone are responsible for your walk; you cannot blame your teacher. When you act from the instructions of others you make someone else's mistake, so you learn nothing. The intent from your Miwi is always good. If you come from deep inside here and you make a mistake then from this comes the greatest teaching. You'll remember this lesson for the rest of your life and maybe eternity.

Things are not always as they seem. Ask yourself, 'Am I listening with my Miwi?' The directions for your journey come absolutely from your Miwi. The Miwi is where you get your messages and then it goes up to the computer and the computer goes up to the head and this is where the ego sits and the ego goes, 'Is this message a good or a bad one?' We decipher it and we do it very, very quickly.

While you're sleeping your Miwi is already travelling the route you will take the next day. It comes back to you and as you get up it goes, 'Do not drive to work today.' Now, you can't very well ring up your work and say, 'Well, my Miwi says no so I am not coming to work.' So instead you tell a little lie. You say, 'I can't come to work today because I'm not very well.' Your Miwi is saying, 'Stay home, stay safe.' Many, many times things have happened to every person reading this because you've got a warning and the ego goes, 'Nah, don't listen. Don't be silly! You're just being really silly!' Then you go, 'OK, ego, yeah, yeah.' So you get in the car and what happens? Your Miwi is going, 'No, don't do it. Danger, danger, bugeenge, bugeenge, bugeenge!' We have an accident and then we go, 'Well, I won't do that next time.' The next week it happens again, then the next month, and again a year later. We haven't listened to our Miwis. Our egos have dictated, 'No, no this is really being silly, you've got to go. You've committed yourself so you'll lose face. Don't you want people to like you?' We have spent our entire lives wanting people to like us when we don't like ourselves. Fear of not being liked has consumed us.

An easy way of explaining to children how to listen to our Miwis is to draw a picture of a Miwi with feelers and little eyes (*see Illustration 8*). Then say, 'You know, your Miwi has little eyes and little feelers and can go out and see if it's safe for you then come back and give you messages. They could be "No, yucky, yucky, yucky. Don't stay here, don't do that, don't climb that big high wall because you'll get hurt! Go home now or Mum'll be mad!" Listen to these messages!'

That's what you need to teach your children so they know how to stay safe. Don't write on their fingers! Little kids only have five bloody

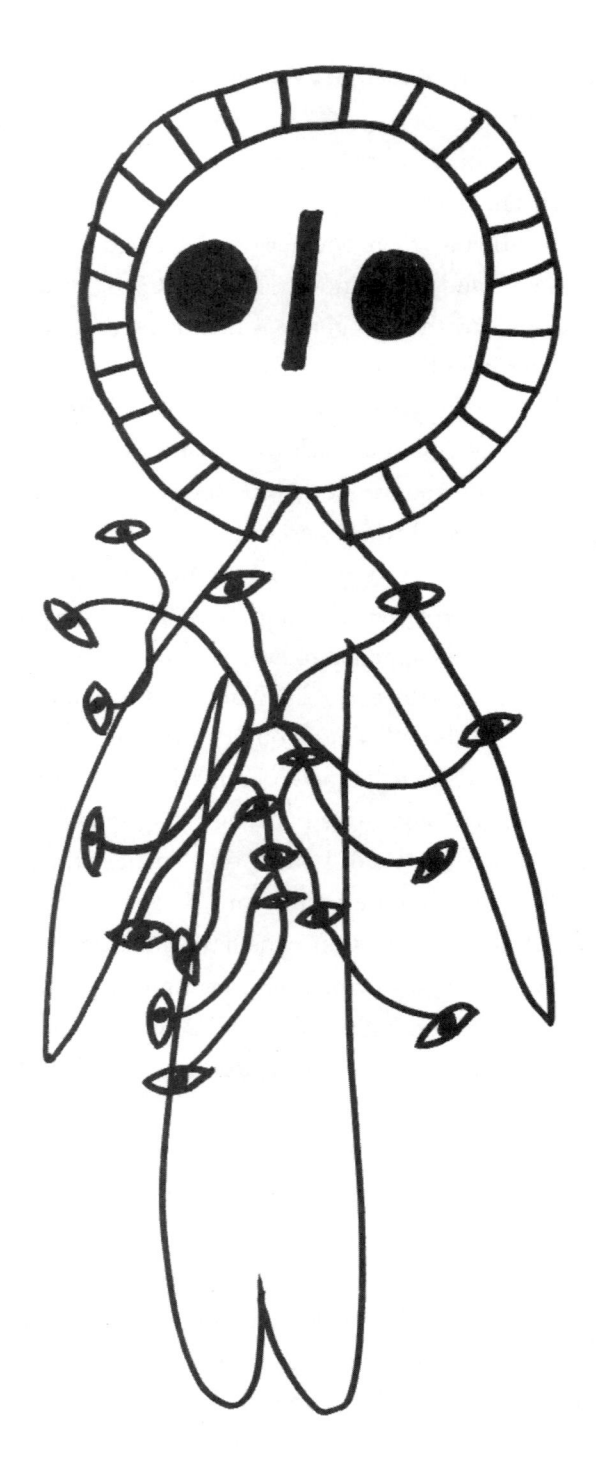

Illustration 8. *Miwi with Feelers and Eyes.*

70

fingers on one hand, so they go, 'Don't do 1, don't do 2, don't do 3, don't do 4, don't do 5'... abyss!! Also don't teach them that if someone is hurting them tell 1 Mum, 2 Dad, 3 Aunty, 4 Teacher, 5 Granny because if no-one listens then again — abyss. Teach them, 'Your Miwi has all these little eyes and it'll come back and it'll tell you, "No, no!" If you don't listen it'll make your legs shake, it'll make your tummy sick.' It is the same with all of us. It's just such a great way of understanding and there's no abyss.

The Miwi Print

Everybody on this planet has a unique fingerprint, hair print and DNA. (For the moment I'll exclude identical twins because that's a separate teaching.) And, everyone on this planet has a unique Miwi print and this holds the coded instructions for our life's journey and our chosen teachings, all billions of us. The prints are like thin films of plastic on top of the placentas. Our journey and the instructions are already written on these, they are sacred, and the one who guides us is Nungeena-tya.

So when a child is born, and the placenta is buried, that Miwi print goes into Nungeena-tya. The placenta is extremely rich so it nourishes her. The Earth needs nourishment as much as we need nourishment. It is a two-way thing. It also honours the Earth by placing the responsibility for our child's journey in her. The Miwi print just lies there for twelve to fourteen years, until that child spills seed. As it hits the Earth, the seed is recognised instantly, almost as if it enters a computer data system. Nungeena-tya then goes back to wherever the Miwi print was buried and locks it in. She then acts to ground and guide the 'wanai' on her journey throughout this physical life.

Can you imagine a mother forgetting any of her children? Would she recognise her children, all of them? Of course! On first sight she would recognise them instantly. That's absolutely true. Nungeena-tya can recognise every single one of us instantly because she's got our print. She knows her children and when they've been born back to her. So as soon as the seed spills, she knows — and it's like a very strong magnet on a fridge. Nungeena-tya grabs and anchors you in. She takes your Miwi and guides you. You start your journey. This is when you start receiving your teaching and learning the lore/law.

Things have changed in recent times. Now we give birth to our babies in hospitals where often the placentas with the Miwi prints go down the rubbish chute with four or five others to be burnt, melting them together. If not, then usually other things are done with them that still melts them together. Eventually they do go back to the earth and Nungeena-tya does take them and recognise them. However, if you take all the fingerprints, hair or DNA of different people then mix them all together and burn them, who would be able to separate all the fingerprints, hairs or DNA again? No-one could.

Perhaps you know someone who has children who have been just divine up until twelve or thirteen years old, never had a problem, they were loving and wonderful. Then when they hit puberty they went ballistic — shaving their heads, drawing swastikas. You can bet your bottom dollar that they were born in a hospital where the placentas were all burnt together because this is what happens to babies who have been born in hospitals when they hit puberty. It's the time when they should be sent on their journey, guided by Nungeena-tya — but their Miwi prints have melted together with the prints of the other babies born in the hospital at the same time. So instead they are confused. Nowadays you see young people living in such stressful ways, tearing in this direction and tearing in that direction, not knowing where they're going. They're really spiritually and emotionally confused and can't fulfil their journey. They have picked up the essence of someone else's journey, they try and they know it's not right; some even end their journeys because they can't fulfil them. It's no one's fault, it's absolutely nobody's fault if this happens. We all have the choice to end our journey, no matter what; the only thing is we have to come back and do it again.

To lose your spiritual map is like being in a rowboat and having to get from one side of a massive lake to the other. There's a storm coming, you've lost the oars and you have to get across using your hands. Your hands are no match for the storms. You get tired rowing the boat with two little arms. From the exhaustion your boat just spins and spins, often you lose direction and go backwards. You might give up and die, you might commit suicide. You don't know your journey. You've got no instructions.

Can you imagine how sad it is for someone to have spiritual Alzheimer's? When the old people used to home birth even without ceremony the placenta was placed in the ground. Nungeena-tya benefited — there were far fewer suicides. You hear a lot of old people today saying, 'Why are the young ones so lost? We weren't like that.' Of course they weren't, because most likely when they were born at home, their placentas were buried one by one in the garden.

Many, many years ago every single culture performed a birthing ceremony. It's everything; the most vital part of one's journey. It is the way people welcome and set you up for your growing in the world. Other cultures may not have understood or done it the way we did; but even a birthing ceremony done with unconscious spirit takes care of a kind of balance. Italian women, Spanish women, Indian women, Koori women, women, women, women, they would birth their babies, nurse their babies and bury the placentas. So there was and is far more grounding in old people. Even today if you see babies or young children who have been home-birthed and their placentas buried in the garden, you'll notice these children are very different. They're very calm and always drawing others to them. They go through normal puberty rather than spiritual lostness and usually have few problems. So they become guided wanais. They might fall down; there are storms, even hail, many diversions pulling them away; bugeenge pulling them away from their teaching and their journey. But when they fall down or get knocked down Nungeena-tya will anchor them and pull them back up. They will always be very, very close to their path if not right on it. These children struggle through to become good and responsible adults. However, if the placenta has been burnt and melted together with other placentas it doesn't get destroyed. It still goes into the earth but because it's melted together it carries the print of the other Miwi prints with which it was burnt — so there's confusion. The Miwi will have more than one map and it really can't connect to its journey. Rebirthing can repair this as can a very close spiritual connection to your guides.

Singing, prayers and spiritual disciplines can reveal your journey but it is still like finding your way from A to B when the most direct route has been destroyed. You then go from A to B, picking up the threads of empathy, swimming the River of Sorrow. And if you give up and stop kicking your arms and legs, you will only drown in the River of Sorrow. On every journey we have to swim the River of Sorrow — it runs on a bed of grief.

There is a piece of protective armour that's embedded into the spirit that does not need a Miwi print to guide it. This is faith — faith in the Creator and the Oneness. I was birthed properly but I think I use faith more than I lock into my Miwi print. I don't concentrate on my Miwi print. I come from the knowing of the Creator and Oneness. That's where I come from with everything. I accept, without question, that the trees have as much right to be here as me, that no animals should be tied up or caged, that no hermit crab or any creature should be trapped in a bowl or a cage for children's amusement just so their parents can watch their favourite TV show. Faith in the Oneness just means that I don't ever want to be apart from the Oneness.

You need to illuminate your path but instead you find yourself stumbling in the dark with one little light, hoping that you're on the path and hoping to get from A to bloody B without falling down a crevasse, or whatever. It's very difficult, but you're doing it on your own, because you think you don't need anything or anybody. So off you go, 'Aaargh!' You've gone into the blackness. Now if you come together with your friend's Miwi, your mother's Miwi, your partner's Miwi and others' Miwis — light, light and light; coming together with everything that has light energy, the birds, bees, trees and the mountains — honouring the light. Now look at the light on your path. The Oneness of Creation is amazing. Being part of or separated from — which way would you travel?

As you know, when a baby is born the placenta is still attached to the child but it still carries the Miwi print of that life's journey. The moment that baby sucks its first breath of air, a switch is flicked, signalling to the map-carrying placenta, that it and the baby are about to be separated. The placenta then ejects its seeds of instruction — how to follow the map — by pumping for about ten minutes through the umbilical cord to the baby. It is important, not only to your baby's journey but to life itself, that the beginning of all Miwis' journeys are not interfered with. There is a great need to have a nominated person there, usually the grandmother, who has been instructed to ensure that no medical personnel cut the cord until it has stopped pumping and is completely still. Only then has the placenta finished pumping the seeds of instruction; this is the Miwi essence. If the cord is cut while still pumping then the cord and not the baby will have the Miwi essence instructions. Doctors use the cords for many purposes and this is OK if the cord is only cut when completely still so it has let go of the baby's Miwi. If done when it's pumping it is like spiritually blinding our babies and hence we have all sorts of new emotional and psychological disorders in children like Attention Deficit Disorder. Fortunately there are many parents who keep the clip and the umbilical cord as a keepsake; this is as good as the original placenta for rebirthing.

Rebirthing

For those of you who are thinking, 'Oh God! I didn't know about this but I want to do it!' there is good news! You can be rebirthed. You can do it for yourself and for others in your life. You can't come up with the placenta but you can come up with two elements that make up the print of the placenta — blood and hair. One carries half of the journey print and the other carries the other half, so you'll get as close as you possibly can. It's good to do the ceremony close to the birth place of the person being rebirthed but this is not absolutely necessary if it's too difficult.

Rebirthing Ceremony

To conduct a rebirthing ceremony this is what you need to do:[11]

- You will need some blood (on a tissue or cloth) maybe from a scratch, fall or knee scrape and a little bit of hair of the person if you do not have the placenta or a piece of the umbilical cord.

- Ask Nungeena-tya to give you a stone that will represent the placenta and don't be surprised if you've got to walk for six months. You'll know it without a doubt when the stone says 'hello'. That's the stone to use.

- Follow your Miwi to choose a location, as close as possible to where the birth was, to conduct the ceremony.

- Dig a hole in this place.

- Gather leaves or natural substances appropriate for cleansing and smoking. In Australia, if possible use sacred gum — it is the most powerful. These are the leaves florists often use — the silvery discs come off the stem two at a time; the colour is a sage green. Use leaves from old trees as the leaves of the young trees have a higher cyanide content. They give off the same kind of purification as sacred water. (There are also other varieties of sacred gum.)

- Take off your shoes.

- Light a fire.

- Take a twig of gum leaves, kneel down on the earth and tap the ground with it. Call Nungeena-tya to ask permission to do the ceremony, saying, 'Nungeena, Nungeena, Nungeena-tya this is your daughter _____. I come to rebirth _____.

- The person conducting the ceremony and any helpers first pass themselves through the smoke to purify themselves, their intent and take away all their negative energy so they are involved in the ceremony coming from a place of light. Saying 'I see no bugeenge, I speak no bugeenge, and I hear no bugeenge' and bringing the smoke towards you with your hands, turn around while the smoke is fanned towards you and say, 'And I do no bugeenge.'

- Then everybody participating is smoked.

- The person conducting the ceremony puts the blood and hair on the stone and passes it through the smoke for cleansing and then burns the hair and blood together on the stone. The stone is placed face down in the earth in the hole already dug.

- Each participant then takes the twig used at the beginning of the ceremony, kneels beside the hole and makes a commitment, one she has every intention in her heart of keeping, to support this Miwi's journey spiritually, emotionally or physically. It can be a very small commitment or even a wish, request or prayer. Once you have made the commitment, bend the twig until it snaps.

- Burn the twigs on the fire so that the commitments travel on the smoke to the Rivers of the Dreaming. If you don't carry out your commitment, you are in deep trouble. When the smoke goes up you're calling on the Creator, or whoever or whatever you hold most sacred, to witness the ceremony.
- Cover the earth over the stone and request Nungeena-tya to accept this rebirthing and to accept the symbolic placenta and for the Miwi's journey to start. Say, 'Guide, anchor and make this one a good, strong, earth-connected Miwi.' Ask for the courage, compassion, wisdom and love this spirit will need.
- At the end of the ceremony hold hands, forming a circle with the person who buried the stone in the middle. Symbolically offer up this rebirthing to the Creator by stepping forward and lifting your arms saying, 'Biami, our birthing'. Then step back and bend down to the earth, offering your birthing to Nungeena-tya and saying, 'Nungeena, our birthing.' Then stand erect and step to the right saying, 'Her journey' and then step to the right again saying 'Her journey'. Then put your weight on the left foot saying, 'Anchor it' and then your weight on the right saying, 'Anchor it'. Repeat this eight times.[12]

It doesn't matter what belief system you follow, this ceremony doesn't conflict. It's not a threat; it is just a rebirthing ceremony to your mother, no more and no less. If you look at present-day Koori society destruction is coming from within because most Koori women are now having their babies in the hospitals and the placentas are being destroyed. There are many, many ways that destroy this kind of teaching. The teachers and the teachings are being lost. Many have said, 'No, no, no, no, this is the devil's way and we are Christians now.'

The Miwi

Miwi is better known as your spirit or your soul. This is not to be confused with Wandjina or Mimi. If I cut you open with a tin opener and look at you inside, this is what's on the journey. Some call it spirit, some call it soul, and some call it essence or God validated within,

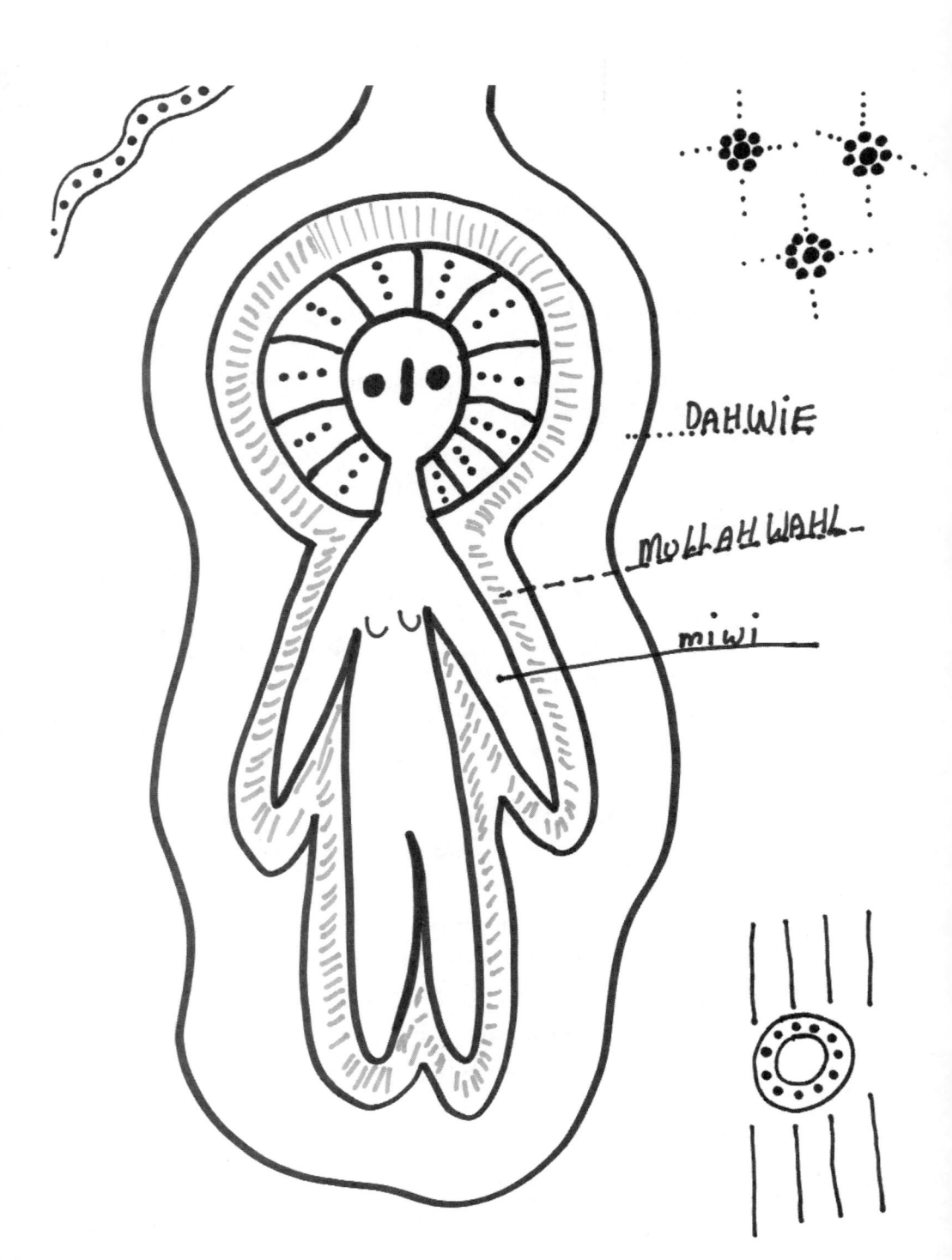

Illustration 9. *Miwi with Dahwie and Mullawahl.*

developed or revealed. The Miwi sits above the navel and under the heart; it pulses and keeps the heart beating. The physical body is really nothing. Our body is only to assist us to physically fulfil our learning tasks. When your shoes are worn out what do you do? Buy another pair.

Now, when you look at an illustration of the Miwi what do you notice as soon as you see it? What's most obvious? Something is missing that gets us into trouble. There is no mouth. If you can afford to get a full body Kirlian photograph done then do this, because it captures the spirit essence and you'll be able to clearly see that the mouth doesn't show up. This is because the Miwis are the 'doers'; they're not the 'talkers'. They just walk, no talk. This makes Miwis so powerful in essence; they are the spirit of everything. So in all Koori teachings the lore/law is 'you walk your talk'.

Everything that came after the Rainbow Serpent has the colours of the serpent. So your Miwi is multi-coloured and covered by a solid sheath called the mullawahl. This is very strong, like Tupperware. It is like little threads of light spirals. The mullawahl gives protection to the inner self against bugeenge — negative spirits. The dahwie then goes right around and expands in and out. The dahwie is soft, almost like a gossamer sheath where the light contains its own light and it is open. The dahwie can open and close and tap into the universal light of the Creator in order to give us strength, protection, the fulfilling of our prayers and the power to heal. Your dahwie picks up energy from the Divine Universe and regenerates itself. For protection we can put blue white light around and seal ourselves off or take the blue-white healing light down to the Miwi, expand ourselves and send it out. The light comes in and out of the dahwie. Negative energy can penetrate and put holes in our dahwie and our Miwis will weaken and weaken until the body dies. This is what happens with 'pointing the bone'. We need to be very careful. However, if we always have an open heart and are kind we are protected.

Miwi Energy

Light a tea candle and place it in a glass. Within this glass you hold a Miwi. This is the light of life. It is someone's spirit, and it's very, very vulnerable. We know how very quickly death can come upon us. Life can be snuffed out in seconds. Our light is vulnerable and delicate. It needs to be cared for and it needs protection. The spiritual forces that we go against are enormous — winds, raging seas — amazingly severe attacks from all areas. This little Miwi light would not survive for a second if you blew into the glass. So what we need is some form of protection. And the Miwi has these two sheaths for protection.

The mullawahl with spirals is the first sheath and like a balloon it can expand. Imagine you are a devoted Catholic, walking along the street and you see the Pope. This amazing energy comes from you, just comes out to meet this force that has such a powerful impact on you. That's how your light meets light. For the Buddhists, imagine seeing the Buddha. Your being would open and go out because, you know, this is it. This is something you never thought you'd ever live to experience and so you open, this is the opening, this is the expanding part.

The light from Miwi energy can be spread, spread and spread. Everyone who works with light knows what they are capable of doing with light — the hands of healing. Just experiment for a minute. Concentrate on imagining blue-white light and place your hands together. Just have your fingers barely touching. Now move the energy really gently back and forwards and think 'blue-white light'. Feel the heat! Every person has their own power. You can test this with somebody. Put your hand close to the nape of her neck, not touching, and it's only a matter of time before she feels the heat.

There it is and it comes back and touches you. It's the powerful energy from your mullawahl, and it's incredibly powerful. It can heal, it can hurt and it can suck. Healers draw on light. For example, Reiki is a very good healing. It does work and it's amazing.

We were born with two hands. Not to get things done better — that's rubbish. You've seen people with one hand who are as adept as we are with two. We were born with two hands because one is for giving and the other for receiving. If you use one hand all the time and you don't use the other it becomes atrophied and you can't use it. This is what we do when we are being martyrs — and a lot of us are martyrs. Instead, when we are receiving we need to accept. It can be really difficult just to say, 'Thank you, you've made my day.' We need to be able to think, 'I am entitled to be spoilt by someone because I'm special. I have this special light. I'm worthy enough that someone will spoil me. I'm worthy that someone will love me.' Then you can become a mirror. Our Miwis can be mirrors. Once you take this on, your Miwi reflects light right out — you just give it out.

Divining Miwi Energy

We can use water divining rods to show Miwi energy. Go to the hardware store and get two pieces of wire (each 20 centimetres long) and two pieces of pipe (each 6.5 centimetres long). Put the wire through the pipe and bend it at 90 degrees so the pipe forms the handle. Hold the divining rods in your hands and think about people you know who give off the most light. Watch what happens to the rods.

You could get a group of people together, and choose the one that you think is the most 'wired up'. Stand about 4 metres away and, holding the rods, ask the person you have chosen to walk towards you. As soon as her energy, her Miwi force, hits, the rods turn in and cross each other. The wires will go as if you've hit water. Then choose someone from the group who you think is your average, everyday person, who gets on with life, who is happy-go-lucky and doesn't worry much, maybe goes to church on Sunday, says the odd prayer, or maybe concentrates on Spirit.

The first person's uptake before the rods might not even be 33 centimetres; she will come very close before the rods move. The second person would possibly be 1 to 2 metres away. Maybe others who pray or meditate daily could move the rods from halfway across that room — not bad. And if someone can get movement from right across that room, they're OK. With the Dalai Lama's light the rods would probably move from a few rooms away. It's what you bring in from the Universe.

The Miwi is just liquid light. We have thirteen major light spots and through these the Miwi's light energy flows within our body and comes out radiating like a pool or a bubble. Your serpent line starts from the base of your skull and ends at the junction that is a spiral anticlockwise just above your coccyx. Then it shoots right down to the ground where you can discharge negative energy and recharge positive energy from Nungeena-tya.

People don't realise the importance of going with no shoes. It is the most effective way to discharge and recharge, especially for children. Try this when you're really, really angry or if your children are off their faces — just go out with no shoes on. Take your children's shoes off and make them walk around the yard. Within minutes the negative energy is discharged, balance is restored and so is calm. Children should never have shoes on when they are playing in their backyard and parents should walk without shoes on the earth for ten minutes, at the very least, every day. I mean earth not bloody concrete, tiles or bricks. They have no life. Anything man-made carries man's garbage, especially when Westerners have made them because most have never been taught to sing up good energy when making something. Instead they pour all their emotional shit into what they are making. This is not saying that Kooris don't have emotional shit — far, far from it. However the older ones have been taught to sing up what they're doing. They work in a meditative state. Watch old people painting their stories. Absolute chaos can be going on around them — kids fighting, people screaming — it doesn't enter their song.

We have major light junctions in our body and light spots over the entire foot because the light begins and ends in our feet. There are two light spots on the inside of the arms above the wrist that are often used in acupuncture, I think. Acupuncture sometimes works excellently but people say, 'Acupuncture, phooey', probably because their light spots have been missed. Run your finger very, very lightly up an arm, even your own arm, make sure it's just brushing, and you'll sense a small dimple. There's a light spot in each one. If it's missing, if it's cold, the light is not flowing somewhere in the body.

Massage should be healing but how many of you have just gone and had a massage thinking, 'I just am so stressed and sore, I've gotta have a deep massage.' Did you listen to your Miwi; did you check out the masseur? Was the masseur safe? Could she possibly have been a spiritual parasite, sucking away your energy? It can happen. So what happens when you get someone who is bugeenge? They go into your body through the dahwie then they puncture the mullawahl, so holes, holes, holes. You get up from your massage and you walk away leaking light. Then for days and days you think, 'Why am I so tired? Why am I so drained? Why do I feel so awful?' Make sure you listen to your Miwi before you have a massage. It's important that we take care of ourselves and protect our Miwis. No doubt you've been with people and then you go home feeling very drained, absolutely sucked completely dry. We can come under attack and people can penetrate. We get holes in the dahwie all the way through to the mullawahl and our light leaks out. So, beware!

What Connects the Miwi to the Journey

Our Miwi's journey is the only thing we're responsible for. It is really important to listen to our Miwis, especially now as there are negative forces everywhere and all our warnings will come from above the navel and under the heart. Regardless of our religious understanding we can be thinking as we walk into a room, 'I could cut the air with a knife.' Our Miwi is saying, 'Bugeenge, bugeenge, back out!' Or we can meet someone and think, 'Oh no!' We've never met them before but there's danger, danger! They're so damaged, so negative, they're so filled with the negative force that you've got to protect yourself.

Perhaps this is a better way of explaining it. Feelers go out from the mullawahl and go through the dahwie. The mullawahl essence travels too; the dahwie has an opening they can go through and go out and test. So it tests: safe? No, danger — bugeenge; back out! That's the warning. Sometimes we don't listen, we don't 'back out' and then we wonder why the consequences are so catastrophic. We're literally in a battle zone of learning and teaching and there's lots of forces against us and what happens is that we get our Miwis covered in silt that, because of blind trust, we take into our essence, our Miwi. Remember it is your right to change your mind if things feel wrong. You need make no excuses; your Miwi knows. Being in the moment is the only place we can be on our journey. A smell can bring you into the moment or take you back to a past life. The senses aren't about the physical, they are directly attached to our Miwi. They manifest in the physical and they can bring us back to the moment, help encapsulate the moment.

Exercising Your Senses

To exercise your senses try this. Go to a fabric shop and buy some little samples of fabric, all different colours but the same texture. Find yourself a sitting place. Don't look as you put the samples in a little bag. Still don't look, but reach into the bag and pick out a piece of fabric. Sit, don't open your eyes, and feel. 'What colour is this?' Just gently roll the fabric in your fingers and feel. Every colour has a different temperature and your Miwi can pick it up. If you know a blind person give her a piece of fabric and ask, 'What colour is this?'

Repeat this exercise for yourself using fabrics of different textures and as you roll them gently in your fingers ask yourself, 'Is this cotton? Is this silk? Is this felt? Is this polyester? Is this nylon?' If you hold something too hard you can't read it. With these fabrics you'll get to know which have come from plants and have a Miwi and which are synthetics and don't. Trust me, you'll know.

The purpose of exercises like this is to make you trust your Miwi and go back to one of your ancient senses that we have almost forgotten how to use — our sense of touch. Once we come back to our true sense of touch different colours will feel either cool or warm, textures will feel different and your knowing will tell you whether the fabric is from living fibre or not.

We have to retrain ourselves to come back into self and trust self. It is no longer safe to blindly trust others to give us true information on many aspects of life. We need the wisdom of discernment and therefore more and more to rely on true self, our inner being. So we have to come back and retrain ourselves. Think of people in country areas who can smell rain days before it comes. Watch the ants; they have not lost their skill. Before the big rains come they carry their babies up trees 12 to 15 metres high. Their very survival depends on this skill and so does ours.

Intimacy

Now we're going to look at intimacy. Do we really know the pure essence of intimacy? No, we don't. Because to have the pure essence of intimacy is to really know something. Through really knowing country — every bump, lump, waterway, plant, tree, animal, insect and puddle — once we are birthed and our seed hits the ground at puberty there is no way we can stray from our path. We simply continue our journey held in the arms of Nungeena-tya. How could we stray?

After doing the suggested exercise you may think, 'What's fabric got to do with intimacy?' Everything, because we're practising on safe things in order to understand; empathising in order to get to intimacy. And it's safe. Because there's no harm done if you open your eyes and think, 'Oh! I thought it was the blue fabric but it's green. Bugger!'

This exercise also teaches you that we are imperfect; we are fragile. It's OK to be imperfect. It's OK to make a wrong judgment, there's always a treasure in everything; there's always a teaching. If you look for the reward in everything then it is the next step on your path. It hasn't become the depressing burden of 'I have failed'. We fear failure but fear is really a wasted emotion. We fear we're going to do the wrong thing. So by becoming intimate with safe things like pieces of fabric, without fear, we can take intimacy further. Then we can practise on living things like trees. It's really a minefield when you're dealing with the vulnerability of people and their ego, pride and vanity.

Remember though, it's not the Miwis of people that are fragile; they're very strong. Your Miwi always tells you and your Miwi is never afraid. There's a difference between giving direction and being fearful. The Miwi guides you. Fear builds in your head — the unfounded fear that we could spiritually die. So we become too afraid to do anything. This fear will spiritually cripple us. It just chases itself around and builds enormous pictures in our mind — pictures of hatred. Hatred is fear. In fact, usually hatred is fear wearing ignorance's clothes and sitting in intolerance's chair.

Envy is also just fear again in disguise. We need to look at fear. We don't like to let people know that we're afraid and we don't want to look at our fears because they seem too enormous. So we need to look at Miwi guidance compared to fear if we are to connect and stay connected to our path. Our Miwis do guide us. You know that

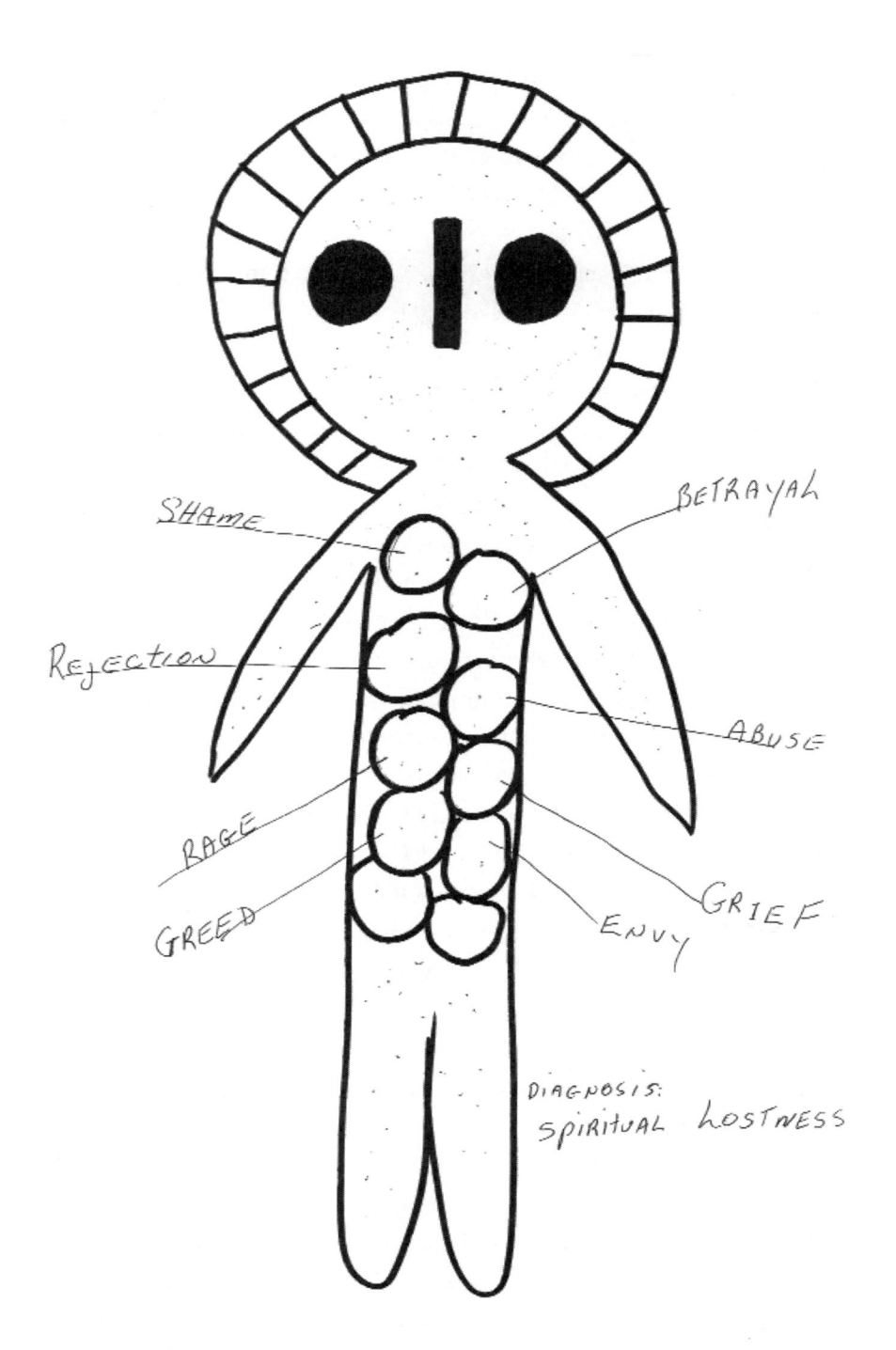

Illustration 10. *Miwi with Pollution.*

feeling you get in your Miwi when you are about to go somewhere that's not on your path, that feeling of 'No, no, bad' — it's the ancient knowing sense.

What Disconnects the Miwi from Its Journey

The ancient knowing sense has been totally dishonoured. Now things are ruled by using our computer — head logic. So we have our computer and we can't get by without it. This gives direction to our Miwis; then we act but we should go from our Miwis. If we don't we keep going through and through the same thing time and time again without learning. The head's computer says, 'What the hell, I'll do it.' And Miwi goes, 'No no, don't go there today.' Then the head says, 'Don't be silly, GO.' And you go and do it. But Miwi knows all along something bad would happen. Go from Miwi, where you pick up your sensors — on your partner, on your children, on every single thing — and you'll be on your journey.

Because the Miwi is centered above the navel, if someone comes to you and you feel betrayal this is the place it hits. The area around the navel goes 'argh'. The feeling reaches all the way to the soul/spirit. This is soul/spirit pain. You're told about a death in the family — 'argh'. It happens every time you are devastated and you almost feel as if a hand is pulling your guts out.

Remember the storms we go through on our journey, all the bugeenge forces against us — these can pollute our Miwis. They can get terribly polluted. Silt and pollution build in the Miwi just through everyday living. For example, think of that rude person in the fruit shop or the butcher's who snarls every time you walk in, or the secretary in the doctor's office who thinks she's 'Princess Leah' and demands to know why you are two minutes early or two minutes late and why your child's nose is running. Those females you work with who have thrown away their 'Red Door' or 'Lulu' perfume and replaced it with the latest 'Bitch Essence'. You put on a party for your husband's colleagues, their wives and children and they all walk out, don't say goodbye, and leave you the washing up. Our Miwis become contaminated; they collect all the bugeenge, the negative energy.

WATER IN THIS DIRECTION NO MORE THAN SIXTEEN METRES

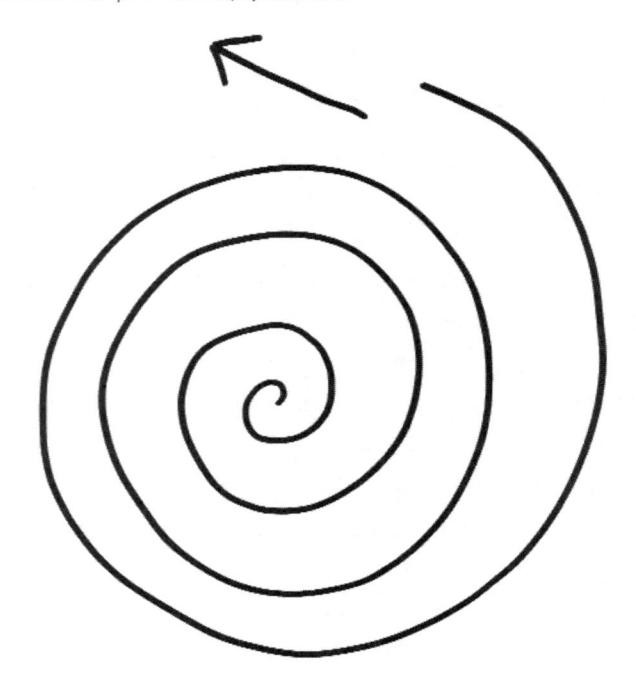

THIS IS ANOTHER EXAMPLE. (MICHALS NOFFITY ")
THIS ONE WOULD BE almost UNDER YOUR FEET

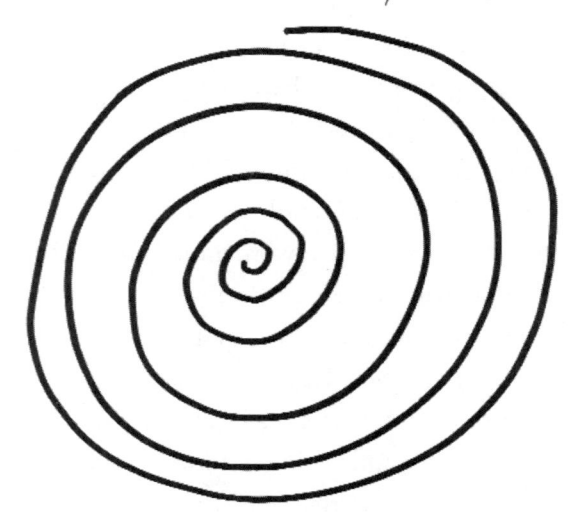

Illustration 11. *Sacred Water Spring Location.*

We have been taught that unless something is solid, it doesn't exist. So don't take my word that this happens to your Miwi, go to a psychic fair where there is Kirlian photography. Before you have the first photo taken go and sit, think about grief, betrayal or sorrow. Think, then touch and feel these emotions. Now go and have a photo taken. Sit again and think, touch and feel blue-white light from the source. 'Ah, blue-white.' Then go and have your photo taken again. Now look at them both. You will see the difference in the two photographs. The first one will be murky just like the sky when you are landing at San Francisco or Heathrow airport — pea soup with a flash of colour. The second will have less murk and more reds, gold and pinks.

Every time we get angry and every time we get negative, a little bit more pollution builds up in our Miwis. They become so dark and gloomy that people can say, 'We don't want to be around you right now.' This is how it happens. We have our light source and we have light flowing all the time; our Miwi is a depthless source of light. But perhaps abuse as a child has formed a boulder within our light flow, then grief another boulder, then boulders of betrayal, humiliation and rejection. I could go on and on. Our light source should flow but it can't. So we suffer depression and mental illness. Diseases — like cancer and diabetes — start within the Miwi; they all show within the Miwi, years before there are any physical manifestations. They manifest because our light can't move and our organs won't function without light.

We can crack open the boulders. The pain can be enormous when we are touching our grief and betrayal. We hang on to them because other people don't want to listen to our sorrow and pain. We despair until we find a good pair of ears with legs. But when we do we can heal ourselves. Once the boulder is broken and the light penetrates, it immediately begins to shrink and heal. And if we have another opportunity with a good listener, the next one will begin to shrink and before you know it the light starts moving. You can touch back in on what is good and this then starts to deal with the grief and betrayal. You can move forward again.

Our Miwis can be washed but only with sacred water. So what can we do? Cry? Absolutely! We don't just have tear ducts because they're a second bladder. No, they're not. Tears and urine are sacred water and they wash the Miwis clean. Sacred water comes from the womb of Nungeena-tya. Any water that has never been touched by sunlight is sacred water. Babies grow in sacred water. Get some water from springs. Look for the symbol in the drawings in *Illustration 11* on page 88; you'll see it carved on rocks.

From *Illustration 11* you can tell which direction the spring will be in. The width of the space at the end of the spiral will indicate to you how far in the direction, in this case I would say about 16 metres. You need to collect the water at night, untouched by sunlight. Bateau Bay has a good spring. I used to go there; I'd collect the water and store it under cover. Sacred water works — drinking it and bathing in it — but you can't beat good old crying. It gets rid of all of the bugeenge or negative energy that attracts more bugeenge.

What Keeps the Miwi Connected

When you take drugs or alcohol into the system the Miwi becomes dazed and it starts to shrink; the dahwie can then easily tear. So if you want to stay connected to your journey, stay clean.

When we begin to cry we start to flush our Miwis clean. Then the voice of our conditioned, lost, Western mind — our computer mind — says, 'You can't cry. It's weak to cry and it's wrong to cry and you should really be strong!' How many times have you said or heard someone else say, 'Stop that crying, right now!' So we stop our crying.

We need to relearn because when you cry your Miwi is being washed — you're vulnerable. Nobody likes to be vulnerable so we do the thing that stops us being vulnerable and stops us crying. The quickest way to stop is rage, become really angry. All this does is put more silt into our Miwi. There's nothing wrong with being vulnerable and we need to become intimate with this.

Miwi Connectedness Maintenance

This is what you can do. Make a cup of your favourite drink or pour a glass of wine (remember, not a bottle) — a treat for yourself. Go and fill the bath up with hot water and if you don't have a bathtub borrow a friend's. Get the water deep and hot; add a little bit of some lovely scented oil like lavender. Light a candle, or even a couple of nice scented candles. Put on some soft music if you like — Enya's good. Just lay back, let the water soak over you, and sip, and sip.

Now I want you to think about your saddest memory or movie. Poor old Lassie — Lassie suffered and suffered and suffered. Think about that movie. 'Who will love my children?' And then I want you to think about 'poor me'. You go 'Lassie', 'Who will love my children' then 'poor me'. By then 'Lassie' starts the welling, 'who will love my children' starts the trickle and 'poor me' starts the flood — wah, wah, wah. It opens the flood gates and you let it go, crying and crying. Or you could think about your favourite singer — Patsy Kline, Kurt Cobain or Michael Hutchence — and how tragic it is that you've missed out, not them, because they died. The suffering you've had to endure because they can't sing any more songs just for you.

Give it half an hour, a good half an hour of this Miwi flushing exercise.

You know when you have a real good cry and you think 'Oh, that's so much better.' Everyone will come home and you'll go 'I love you!' You'll love everybody; you'll be on a natural high because tears have flushed your Miwi clean and drawn the bugeenge, negative energy, away from your Miwi. Flushing also grounds you, keeps you focused and is good for you physically. You think more clearly and you look at things more clearly. You need to do this at least once a fortnight; when you're premenstrual is good. You can do two jobs at the once — cleanse the body and the Miwi. It's important to teach your children, teach your sons, teach your partner, teach everybody — but especially do it for yourself. We need to cleanse our Miwis regularly.

When children start to cry — and remember, crying is good — this 'wah wah' in your face can irritate you. That's all right because you just need to set the scene as I do with my grand-daughter who is a chronic crier. I swear that she still hasn't used her bladder yet because she uses her eyes so much there's been nothing left to come out of her bladder.

Cleansing a Child's Miwi

Take your child to a nice place and say, 'Here's a lovely little place and I'll put some cushions down.' Give her a shiny bright mirror, put it in front her; kids love mirrors. She could pull faces and do all these warped things while she's flushing her Miwi. Don't leave her on her own to cry unless you have the mirror. Then you say, 'Look at your sad little face. Just look at your sad little face. I'll go and get a picnic ready — delicious afternoon tea. You have a good old cry and I'll come back and check on you.'

Later you return and say, 'Do you feel better, baby?'

'Sniff, sniff, sniff,' your child responds.

You get a tissue and you wipe it all and you say, 'I've got a little surprise for you.' So you put them up at the bench and say, 'Here's your little picnic — fairy bread, Milo and your favourite biscuits. Now this will make you feel better.'

Before long, you've got a much better child on your hands. Watch her grow.

You can do this for a baby, two weeks old. Hold the baby in your arms and say, 'Oh, you poor little thing', and she'll cry and cry and cry. You are giving off the energy that allows the crying to be triggered. This is baby Miwi cleansing.

Often mothers feel like they want to murder their two-year-olds — it's just a natural thing. We try to suppress it but we can't. Rather than hit your child, ask her, 'Do you need to have a good cry, sugar? You look so sad. Here's the mirror.' Soon you won't feel the need to smack your children, especially if you are crying and cleansing your own Miwi regularly.

One of the first things we are taught from the old teachings is to find our sitting or thinking place within our own country. Then, when walking in a dreadful storm, unsure of our path, and needing help we can take refuge; we go to our sitting place. We can sit and dwell, we have the essence within. We have our essence, our Miwi within us that's connected to the Oneness. We can sit right down with and be connected to our Mother, Nungeena-tya. Then we are safe. We can call for spiritual guidance instead of crawling into the most immediate psychological cave and hiding away.

We can also go on journeys to seek a Dreaming track where the power of light is so strong and the guides are so focused that we can be guided back to our path. This is similar to the traditions of pilgrimage. People go to Mecca, Lourdes, Varanesi, Llandaff, The Burran, Machupitchu, Bodhgaya, Jerusalem, Glastonbury and many more. In our tradition we go walkabout, moving from sacred site to sacred site, honouring and singing them up. Sacred places have sacred stories. You might go to seek power and guidance from Uluru, Wuuluumbin (where the Eighth Sister sleeps), or Goolooga (Mother of the Stars with Bahloo's wife sitting beneath her), to Kangaroo Valley or Point Plummer (near Port Macquarie) in New South Wales. These are places of profound spiritual energy and they will have an impact on people. Many people go for spiritual guidance and have amazing spiritual experiences finding fulfilment and spiritual release.

Part Two

THE JOURNEY – THE BIRTHING CEREMONY

Do you remember that every person on the planet has a unique Miwi print on his/her placenta and that this holds the instructions for their life's journey? So when you are born your placenta needs to be buried in the earth, in Nungeena-tya, on its own. Then your journey is anchored and your Miwi print waits there until you become a wanai. The placenta nourishes the earth and we are honouring Nungeena-tya by placing the responsibility of our child's journey with her. This is why the Birthing Ceremony is so important to my teaching.

Traditionally, our placentas would be buried near a tree of significance for our tribe. We would know the major songlines of our tribe, our child would have our tribal totem, and we would know their personal songline — their personal totem.[13] So we would know all the songlines that influenced our baby and we would also know all the essences of the trees we might want to plant the placenta near. A tree would be then chosen because it had the spiritual essence that we decided was the one to give to our child. It was a giving of the gift of another essence and another strength for the child to carry through life.

Nowadays I encourage women to plant trees or bushes over the placentas that will be part of the essences that will influence their children. So you need to put a lot of thought into what to plant — think about the positive and the negative qualities of each tree or bush. You can't make the child's journey easier but what you can do is offer a gift of what you think would be of benefit to her. And as the tree grows so does that essence grow within your child.

Really think about what you want for the child or the child's journey — especially if you are the grandmother, because the grandmothers perform the ceremony, and if not them then a chosen great aunt. Normally women need to be over thirty do the ceremonies. Things are changing but still the grandmothers usually do the ceremonies. The day may come when you're a grandmother and you'll be doing the ceremony and you'll take your place in fulfilling this role in a child's journey.

Plant Essences

By the essence of the plant I mean its different qualities and to help you choose I want to discuss some of these. There are many books written about Australian bush foods and medicine trees so have a look at some of them. You could also ask Kooris in your area about the trees that grow near you. You need to learn about the plants before you make the decision.

Now take the Australian **grevillea** for an example.[14] Grevilleas, because of their beautiful nectar, provide nourishment; they also offer shelter because they are strong — they can take some very strong winds. I would say they have a sweet nature. So if you plant a grevillea over the placenta, then what you're wishing for your child is that she will always have friends and company around her. Often the people attracted to her will be looking for shelter and nourishment — for a shoulder to cry on.

There are so many plants and trees in Australia but the **gum tree** is one everyone knows. The gums are the givers of shelter — so people will come to your child for shelter. There are many types of gums — there's the **stringy bark**, the **ironbark** and the **bloodwood**, to name but a few. The **bloodwood** is a sacred tree because when you cut it, it bleeds. The **stringy bark** has very flammable bark and you can make string out of it. So it has in its essence the way for very tight bonding to something. When a forest fire comes and the flames go up the trees, burning straight up and exploding the gases within the top of the trees, it is the stringy barks that have the great honour of being the very first trees out of all the gums to shoot forth new life and produce life-giving oxygen. So it's a matter of knowing about the plants and thinking about what they can do and then you know their essences.

Fig trees are very special because they are the sacred trees of life.[15] So if you choose a fig tree your child's journey will be very 'life journey' focused; you'd be giving the child a real introduction to life and life experiences. But a **sandpaper fig** can easily break in a storm and it has leaves like sandpaper. So it will not be giving your child very much spiritual strength and as the child grows he/she could easily rub people the wrong way.

Lilly pilly trees bear lots of fruit so planting one of these will mean your child will be a nurturer. But if choosing a lilly pilly you will need to be careful that your child won't be 'fed off' by the people around her.

I've mentioned that Biami, our Creator, has a garden in the Rivers of the Dreaming and some of the plants on earth have come from here.[16] There's the **native frangipani**, the **bunya-bunya pine**, the **arran tree** and the **bush orange,** these all came from Biami's garden. So with the choice of any of these trees the baby is going to have to live up to certain spiritual expectations. Think carefully about choosing any of these special trees.

It doesn't seem to matter what culture you come from everybody knows when a particular baby is born that this one is 'an old spirit'. For these babies, put their placentas underneath a **Queensland weeping fig** or a **bunya-bunya pine** — the sacred tree of knowledge. These babies will have knowledge and they will impart knowledge and wisdom. All pines are linked to the tree of knowledge and many ceremonies are held under pines. If you plant a pine, for example a **Wollomi pine**, this will give your child a thirst for knowledge and an appreciation of knowledge — be it spiritual or otherwise.

The spiritual essence of the **oak tree** is that it's strong, shady and protective. Let's consider the **she-oak**[17] — a wonderful tree. It can take great forces of wind before it snaps. The nuts can save people's lives and their juice can reduce the body's dehydration rate by up to 90%. The roots are used for birth control. There's a whole lot of medicinal power around this one tree. So your child would have incredible endurance — real staying power. However, if you're thinking of planting a she-oak over the placenta remember there's a negative side. This wood makes the hottest fire, so you're going to have someone with a very hot temper.

Now the **ti-trees** (or **paperbarks**, as some people call them) are extremely sacred, in that the spirit of every single Kadaitchi who dies enters a ti-tree. So Kooris never ever cut down a ti-tree because if you cut it down you release the spirit guide and you release wrath. Now you must realise there is no spiritual punishment for ignorance, but once you know about this tree then it's a different matter. The ti-tree is a healing tree and it's got healing properties for all kinds of sicknesses. I wouldn't choose it unless it was a male child who you considered extremely special. Some people would but I'd hesitate because the child will always be expected to heal someone else's wounds. I wouldn't put a ti-tree over a female child.

I don't know a lot about imported plants, but let's take one of these, for example, a rose bush. I chose this one because women are often tempted to plant **roses** over the placenta. Roses are considered one of the most beautiful flowers in the world, be it for their spiritual beauty or their physical beauty. They smell gorgeous and they look beautiful. If you plant a rose bush your child will probably have an essence of beauty — she will be a beautiful personality who will draw other energies towards hers. But remember, roses have thorns and can cause injury and they often get thornier as they get older. So when she's growing up and you've got this beautiful angelic child one minute and a prickly cow the next, you will know why. But maybe your child needs to be prickly in order to get by, so follow your Miwi in choosing the plant for your child.

Another tree you may want to consider to plant is a **willow tree**. Willows have properties that are good for medicine and for healing but you must always plant them near water. So if you plant a willow tree your child will probably possess a will that gives and she'll have compassion and empathy.

I hope that you get an idea from these few examples that trees have very different essences and therefore qualities and it's important to know about them before you can make a choice for your child's journey. When you choose you also need to follow your Miwi — what feels right to you, for your child.

The Ceremony

At a Birthing Ceremony the mother, the grandmothers and all the aunties come to celebrate and each one makes a commitment to help the child's journey. Then when the child becomes a wanai and she is starting on her teaching she has many women to ask questions of and who she can go to for support. The husbands of the women in the ceremony become the father and grandfather figures for this child.

I was asked once whether the grandmothers and the aunties would come together beforehand to discuss what commitments they were going to make; traditionally it's never discussed before the Ceremony itself. I believe that when we discuss things we can sometimes make decisions from our desperate need to be liked and approved of, rather than what we need to do for our journey. I always find that as soon as I kneel down to make my commitment, I immediately know what to do and what to give. So for example, say I'm a grandmother making my commitment, I might say, 'This is my grandchild _____. My wish for her journey is to let her journey be strong and straight. My commitment to this child on her journey is that I will always be available to give this child the traditional teachings.' And then an aunty may come along and her commitment to this child may be that she will teach this child about the Creator. So it's important when you do make the commitment that you are honest with yourself and say only what you know you will be able to fulfil. Essentially what you are saying is, 'I will do my very best, physically, mentally and spiritually, but I won't try to be God.' Even though as life unfolds some of these children could grow into adults that could do some very bad things that make you want to walk away and condemn them, YOU CAN'T. If you make a spiritual commitment, you can't walk away from it — it's not about the child as much as it's about your journey and what you commit to do.

Sometimes the commitment may seem like a very simple thing at the time but we don't know what will happen in the child's life; a simple thing may turn out to save the child's life. No one is judged for her commitment and often you don't say it out loud.

How to Conduct a Birthing Ceremony

- A Birthing Ceremony is similar to the Rebirthing Ceremony[18] but for this you need the placenta or a piece of the umbilical cord of the child to be birthed. You will need the tree to plant over the placenta or you need to have chosen the established tree which the placenta will be buried next to. Remember to consider the essence of the tree, its strengths and its weaknesses.

- If you have chosen to plant a tree then you need to decide where to plant the tree and to do the ceremony. It could be in your backyard or a place that is important to your family. Trust your Miwi to help you find the location. Then you need to dig a hole deep enough for the placenta and the tree, or dig a hole next to where the tree is already growing.

- If you are in Australia gather, if you can, the same sacred gum that is mentioned in the Rebirthing Ceremony. If you are elsewhere then gather the natural materials that are traditionally used for cleansing through smoking.

- Light the fire and have one or two people tending the fire for the smoking ceremony.

All those participating need to be barefoot. The participants form a circle with the mother and baby and grandmother inside the circle.

- The grandmother (or chosen great aunty) who is conducting the ceremony takes a twig of gum leaves, kneels down on the earth and taps the ground three times as she calls Nungeena three times, to ask for permission to do the ceremony, saying, 'Nungeena, Nungeena, Nungeena-tya this is your daughter _____. I've come to birth _____.

- Everybody participating is then smoked — to purify themselves, their intent and take away all their negative energy so that they come from a point of light. The fire needs to be smoking, not burning so the helper can pat the flames down with a small branch and fan the smoke towards each person. The grandmother or chosen aunty and any helpers pass themselves through the smoke first. Each one comes close to the smoke and says, 'I see no bugeenge, I speak no bugeenge, and I hear no bugeenge'. As she speaks, she brings the smoke towards herself with her hands first touching her eyes, then her mouth and then her ears. Then she turns her whole body around on the spot as she says, 'I do no bugeenge.' Each of the participants then comes to do this, one by one, and then she walks back to her place in the circle.

- Then the grandmother passes the placenta through the smoke for cleansing. She holds the baby and quickly passes her through the smoke on her belly and then on her back. She hands the baby back to the mother.

Then the grandmother puts the placenta in the ground with the cord up and the Miwi map down and it's covered over with dirt.

- Next, all participants are given a twig of gum leaves and one by one, after the grandmother, they come up and kneel beside the buried placenta. This is when, with strong heartfelt intention, you make a sacred oath — a commitment to support this baby's journey. It can be a small commitment and a wish, request or prayer. You tap the ground three times with your twig as you say, 'Nungeena, Nungeena, Nungeena-tya, this is your daughter _____ I've come to celebrate the birthing ceremony for _____. Let her journey be _____ (e.g. long, happy). May she have _____ (e.g. grace, integrity). And my promise for her journey is that for the rest of my life I will always strive to or do my best to _____ (e.g. laugh together, teach her about the Oneness). Once you have made the commitment, bend the twig until it snaps and place it on the pile next to the hole and walk back to the circle.

- The twigs are now burnt in the fire and the commitments travel on this smoke to the Rivers of the Dreaming. As the smoke goes up you're calling on the Creator, or what it is that you hold most sacred, and all your ancestor spirits to witness the ceremony and your part in it. You could be in trouble if you don't keep your commitment. That's why it's so important to think very carefully before you make it. Remember, this is not about this child's journey; it is about you and your spiritual integrity.

- Next, the tree is planted on top of the placenta.

- Then the women in the circle hold hands, with the grandmother, mother and baby still in the middle. The circle symbolically offers up this birthing to the Creator by stepping forward, with all arms lifted up, saying 'Biami, our baby'. Now the grandmother pours a little earth through the baby's hand. Then the circle, with hands still held, steps back one step and bends down to the earth, offering this birthing to Nungeena-tya saying 'Nungeena, our baby'. Then everyone stands erect and steps to the right saying 'her journey'; they then step to the right again saying 'her journey'; then to the left saying 'Anchor it'; and then to the right saying 'Anchor it.' (Anchor is the best word I could find, but in tradition the literal meaning of the word used is 'grow baby to you grow it up'.) This is repeated eight times.

- To finish the ceremony everyone sings the Nungeena-tya song three times.

It's important to know the Nungeena-tya song because it's the singing up song and it's always sung at the Birthing ceremonies. It's difficult to translate but it's about honouring, and it means, 'Mother Earth, your soul and my soul are eternally linked. I honour you, I greet you Mother Earth.' And it goes like so in my language.

> Gundra ah la oo noo Nungeena-tya
> Gundra ah la oo oo noo
> Yahmah koora
> Yahmah koora Nungeena-tya
> Ya ah mah koo oo ra

Chapter 7

THE JOURNEY – AGE AND RESPONSIBILITIES

From a traditional point of view we come to this teaching place — this planet — for two things: all truth and all knowledge. To be like Biami, our Creator, who is all truth and all knowledge — this is our goal. Oneness, is how we describe it. In the Oneness we honour everything for its differences. Everything comes together and fits so perfectly — we are just one.

There is men's business, women's business and there is our business. Remember that under the lore/law, women are the community developers. We have the hearth — the fire, the home. We give birth to and feed the children. These women's teachings are about the essence of women and our responsibility to ourselves, our families and our community. Women are ruled by the emotions and part of our journey is to become intimate with these. The female is the nurturer, but I don't mean barefoot and pregnant in the kitchen, or outside lumping coal; I mean with the greatest of honour that we were created for a purpose. We are the very first teacher a child has, and the first lesson is about trust and this teaching comes from us, the mothers.

Traditionally the women kept the kinship lines and bloodlines right around the country. There were trading routes that went all over the place and inter-tribal marriages were arranged along the trading routes. This was to ensure there was no inter-breeding or inter-marrying along the bloodlines and for a bloodline to be reconnected. You could never marry someone from a direct bloodline. The exchanges might go like this: say that the Wirradjirri tribe was next door to the Baakandji, and then further up the trade route was the Kimillaroi. If you were born to Wirradjirri then you married into Baakandji, and then your children would marry into Kimillaroi and then your grandchildren to the next tribe and so on up, up and up. For blood to go the full circle around and meet back up again, it could take between 400 and 5000 years. You'd never get a direct blood link — you couldn't marry a cousin even thirty times removed, believe you me! Women were vicious with the keeping of the kinship lines. So they were very clearly kept and we had no inbreeding, no impurities. This all changed with colonisation. Under white law, Indigenous people were seen as 'fauna' and used to relieve male 'sexual tension'; we women were raped, our men massacred and our children stolen. Marriages were arranged by the mission managers' wives and as long as the couple were not brother and sister the only concern was breeding out the colour — so darker was coupled with fairer. The mission managers fathered as many children as they could to assist the lightening process and give their wives respite from their sexual appetites.

It's important to understand that the female essence and the male essence are different. And it's important to learn to validate our differences. Females look different, we think differently, we behave differently and we have different chemicals in our bodies. Differences are really to be celebrated and not to be reined in and controlled. Men and women fit together physically as well as spiritually. In short it's a perfect balance. However, with the breaking of Biami's stones and the energy He is now sending into Nungeena-tya, the energy is coming up through her in the form of the feminine and so women are being given the task of healing the planet. It is also raising the feminine in the men. Men are becoming gentler. There is a drastic reduction in the testosterone production because of the light that's coming into the planet.

I once asked the Tall Ones why the Kadaicha (lore/law men) were given the higher lore/law. They replied, 'Men have the essence of reason; women are vicious, men are cruel. Women have fluctuating compassion. Men don't harbour resentment like women. Women can carry this for many, many lifetimes for the same person. Many lifetimes are disrupted by women trying to get what they didn't have; they are vengeful.'

Traditionally, men are the hunters, the historians and the protectors. They are ruled by the physical and they are created for this purpose. There are times when men must protect the land, the country and all for whom they are responsible. This may result in conflict or war. This responsibility should certainly give us women greater compassion for men.

Unfortunately, today we are moving away from our roles and the result is that our Miwis are beginning to shrivel. I know we're in a really difficult situation and that to pay off a mortgage is like two lifetimes of slogging your guts out. But we need to call a halt to this madness and say, 'OK, we are humanity.'

The awareness starts from self, and then it can go out. This could be the last day of our lives so it's important that we make every day count. We need to come back to our roles. A man can't give birth to a child and a man can't breastfeed. We women were born with a role to do. With the milk from the mother's breast comes light — and also the mother's Miwi intent. We don't have to be superwomen. We don't have to impress other women. We don't have to impress men either. We've become so influenced and controlled by this invisible thing, this keeping up with the Joneses which triggers and feeds our opponents — that is ego, pride, resentment, frustration, envy and fear. It makes us think that if we run fast enough and if we work harder again our opponents are going to disappear. They won't. They're just going to grow and grow. We need to come back to ourselves in our sitting place and look at these opponents.

We need to ask ourselves, 'How do we want Nungeena-tya to be in another 100 years' time? How do we want to see our grandchildren and great-grandchildren — without water, without fish, diseased all over and a mob of spiritual eunuchs?' That's where we're heading and if you have any doubt you live constantly with your head in your arse.

The lore/law is that we are all, men and women, born boss of self. We need to walk our talk. It's that simple. We walk our journey as boss of self and we die as boss of self. We cannot walk somebody else's journey nor sway them to walk ours. They must walk their own.

Nowadays there are a lot of men who are interested in women's teachings, and so I once tried to teach a mixed group but I found it very difficult. I felt ill and I didn't share with the group the sacred Birthing ceremony. It just didn't feel right for me to do it with men there although a lot of the old women say these days that it's fine for men to join in the Birthing ceremony because often men are so much part of the birth of a child. But I don't teach men, I teach women. There are a number of men's business teachers for men who want to follow their vision quest and learn.

There is still a deep respect in Aboriginal culture today for men's and women's business. If you go to a place where you have a ceremony, fair or a Koori gathering you'd be surprised that even the most 'I don't give a shit' type of guy, staggering around, pissed out of his brain, as soon as anyone mentions, 'Women's business going on here' he'll immediately straighten himself up and with not a word walk away, with dignity and absolute respect. I've never ever, in all the chaos that has reigned in Koori communities, seen men disrespect women's business or vice versa. As soon as a woman says, 'Oh, don't come down here; us women are all down here talking', as soon as they hear the words 'women's business' the men go, 'Ooooh!' and they walk away immediately. If a woman is walking somewhere and there is a gathering of men and they say, 'Men's business is going on down here', she'll turn and walk away.

The Story of Dinawahn

A long time ago in the Dreaming there was a young boy. His name was Dinawahn. I'll tell you his story.

Dinawahn was a good young boy, but he didn't like being around the men and he didn't like being around other boys. Every time you turned around, Dinawahn was hanging around the women. They'd go gathering bush tucker and straggling behind would be Dinawahn! The old people started to get concerned about this. They'd say, 'He's a wanai now, he should be starting to go with the men and learning about hunting.' Others would say, 'He should be off with the young boys, growing and learning and unfolding.'

The men would say to him, 'Dinawahn, you need to come with us. You need to learn about this now; you're growing up into a man soon.' Did he listen? No. The women would be off gathering bush tucker and coming up behind them would be Dinawahn. No-one knew what to do. He was getting older and older and they'd say to him, 'Off with the men!' He'd

under the quandong tree

start going off with the men hunting, they'd go to sleep, and he'd creep away and back he'd come and follow the women again!

This became a real concern. The elders and the old clever people spent hours and hours, days and days, months and months, and years and years saying, 'Dinawahn, this is your role. This is what you must do. You must hunt for your family, you must do this and you must do that. This is what you're born to, this is your responsibility.' But as soon as they turned their backs, back he'd go to the women! It started to get very, very dangerous because he was getting older.

Now under the lore/law, and today it's still the same, if a man sneaks up and witnesses a women's ceremony, he is breaking the lore/law. Breaking this lore/law is death. You are sung. You are bone dusted. You're in deep, deep shit. Shit like you wouldn't believe. If a woman sneaks up on a men's ceremony, it's the same. It's very, very clear. There is women's business, there is men's business, and then there is our business. Biami gave us very, very clear roles in the Creation. This is what we've been given. This is our role, this is what we do.

Now the ceremonies were starting and the women got up real early and tried to sneak away from Dinawahn. So off they went, a long, long way away. They were doing the ceremony — and it was one of the most sacred women's ceremonies — when one of the women looked up and, lo and behold, the face coming through the bushes was Dinawahn's. There he was, watching the women's ceremony. All hell broke loose and the women went back to the clever people and said, 'Dinawahn has broken the lore/law'.

Now under the lore/law wanais are not put to death. All the things that happen when they're young, before they're thirty, are about growing and learning their lessons. The best lessons you ever learn are the ones you learn yourself. So you can't put a wanai to death under the lore/law. Finally, the old clever people swung their bullroarer and called Biami down. They said, 'Dinawahn has broken the lore/law, the worst lore/law, and we can't do anything with him.'

Now Biami came down and said to Dinawahn, 'We can't let you do this because you are unravelling the whole of society. You can't go with the women, because you're not a woman. You have a role to fulfil as a man; this is your responsibility. You can't do this because it's against the law/lore. I must teach you and all those who come after you a lesson.'

With that Biami showered a breath over Dinawahn and turned him into a bird, a very big flightless bird; he couldn't fly. He would be that bird for the rest of eternity and so the emu was born. Nearly all birds are the spirits of women, spirits of women that have come back. Birds are the energy, spirit and messengers of women — except for the eagle, hawk and the night bird.

Dinawahn had been irresponsible and shown disrespect for the rights and the roles of others so Biami turned him into a bird. He runs fast and his feathers are like a lap-lap, and they flap like a lap-lap, and he runs to hide his shame. To this very day, the emu is the most inquisitive of all the birds. If you go out in the bush, say to a paddock of emus near Yass, and you lie on the ground on your back, the emus will go around in circles and they'll get closer and closer to you and when they get right up to you that's when you catch them. Grab them and then they're food! Truly! You can't outrun them but you don't have to chase down emu. All you've got to do, if you're ever hungry out in the desert, is lie down on your back and have a big waddi buundi (club) ready, and he'll come up to you. That's not all — the male emu has to be mother for all eternity. He's got to hatch the eggs. The female lays them and then she walks away. The male's got to sit on them and hatch them and then he's got to raise them. You want to be a woman, you be a woman!

This story is a warning for all — men and women — to respect nature's boundaries.

The Five Life Stages

Our business is where we nurture and rear children together. Children choose their mother and father, and our business is where we clearly commit to the lore/law and take up the spiritual contract between the mother, the child and the father to assist each other in learning this life's lessons, for example greed and tolerance. Our business is to honour the sacred together, support each other in our need to do ceremony at our sites. While the men are off on ceremony the women care for the children and feed the men. The men can't feed themselves during ceremony because they cannot hunt. When the women are off on ceremony the men care for the children; the women only take the boodthoongs with them because they are tit fed. Our business is ensuring that together our children get the most important teachings they will ever receive — their role and part in the Oneness.

A child is born with all Miwi knowing and between three and five years of age a veil descends over their spirit memory.[19] Then it's up to the mother to guide the child until she has been taught and understands about 'boss of self', about 'listening to Miwi' and about 'action versus consequence'. Children need boundaries and that's another part of the parents' spiritual responsibility. In infancy the father's main role is to lead by example. You live your spiritual principles into your children. Children absorb these principles by truth and the truth is in your living. How often has your child called you or your partner a hypocrite?

Traditionally there are five stages in our lives.

Boodthoong: from birth to three years old

Under the lore/law, from birth to three years of age, you are a boodthoong — an infant. Traditionally when babies were born they were constantly held, going from one pair of strong arms to another for three years. You're only let down when you struggle to get down. During these years you're carried everywhere by everybody. We say that you are a 'lap dog'. It is different from non-Koori society where you are an 'infant' and at about twelve months, when you start to walk, you are a 'toddler'. In Koori society there's no such thing as 'toddler', you are simply an infant. There are no responsibilities and no expectations during this time.

In traditional society the grandmothers are the prime 'parents'. The grandmothers' roles are so important because we have our babies in our wanai years — before we are thirty, before passion marries reason. The aunties and sister-in-laws are mothers also. So say I am one of four sisters and we each give birth to four children then each of us has sixteen children. At the Birthing Ceremony the Memees (grandmothers and great aunties), the aunties and the mother all make commitments to the baby's journey.[20]

In traditional society there is no such thing as women who don't have children. Under the lore/law, children are not owned by anybody; they belong to everybody. Giving birth does not make a woman a mother. It only means that you have given birth and then you could become a nurturer. You don't have to give birth to a child to be a nurturer for a child can be sent to you by another path. You also become their teacher. So women who don't physically give birth are as important, equal and vital as women who have because there is no difference really. It is usually the women who haven't given birth who know more about the lore/law and often have big responsibilities. Under the lore/law all my sisters' children are my children as much as the ones that I have birthed; there's absolutely no distinction. All my children are their children and they are just as responsible for feeding, washing, teaching and nurturing them in every way.

There's often a misconception about this so people say, 'You know them Kooris, they just give their kids away.' The Memees usually decide where the children go. They are the pivot of society, the matriarchs, and they'll say, 'OK, you know, Gloria that's your one. Take the other one from Valda and give it to Ronnie.' That's what happens and it's good because it's often very hard having one mother. The relationship can become volatile but a child can go to another mother to say, 'I hate Mum, she's horrible' and mother number two can reply, 'OK, lovely, well, you know, come here and I'll tell you this story and then we'll have a treat.' So this kid can go from mother to mother to mother. When all those little monsters are in your ear, and you can't decide where they are and what to do with them there's another mother over there who's not hearing the demons or the same opponents as we are.

Boori: from three to between twelve and fifteen years old

(*Be aware and remember the word is 'BOORI' because if you forget and say, 'BOORAY' you will have called someone's child 'a little fart' — and some black mothers are big!*)

From three years old to about twelve to fifteen years old, under the lore/law, you are a boori — a child. During these years children have no gender responsibilities, and they're non-sexual. They can play with each other's naughty parts to their heart's content. Traditionally children are given special treatment to ensure that they develop a sense of a 'child self'. They are allowed to unfold and grow, just like a flower.

under the quandong tree

They chase crickets and grubs. They make mud pies with flowers in them. They just play. Little girls can play the didgeridoo. It's a matter of allowing them to unfold gracefully, rather than controlling them.

Today, we usually oversee the moulding — not the unfolding — of our children. We have unfair expectations: 'you'll be a scientist when you grow up'; 'you'll go to Cambridge, won't you, sweetie?' Such expectations are put on those who cannot yet spiritually cope with them. Non-indigenous people who work with Kooris, often come to me and say, 'Those Kooris, they let their kids run wild out there!' No, no, they're teaching them — you are born boss of self, you live your journey boss of self, and you die boss of self. They're allowing the children to unfold. It's so important not to shift them away from their journey's path, not to try to take over the Creator's role by deciding when and what our children will be. It won't happen, it has already been decided.

Now if a little girl taunts a little boy, or hits a little boy, he's quite entitled to hit her back, because they're not 'a little boy', they're not 'a little girl', they're simply booris. We usually let them fight it out. There's no gender responsibility put on to them at this age; they are equal. In the development of children it's good that they grow up equal because there's plenty of time later to put gender responsibilities on to them.

Remember, we are born with two emotions that we inherited from the Rainbow Serpent — anger and compassion. You can observe a very young child seeing something hurt and going, 'Oh!' because she has inherited that compassion. In the fighting you observe the anger there too. So forget saying to children, 'There's no such thing as anger!' Children have not yet learnt to temper their emotions or their behaviour. They're simply children needing to learn from their own experience about action and consequence. So we usually don't get into our children's fights, we leave them alone to sort it out. They are not going to die from a bloody nose, black eye or a busted lip. They're learning you can't just hit someone without consequence. If they don't experience the consequences of their actions they can become cruel to animals, babies, other children and may even grow up to commit murder.

Between three years old and five years old a veil descends and then lifts again just before death. This veil closes the door on past and future life memories. It closes the door on the ability to see and communicate with spirits unborn, for example past relatives and unborn babies. However, if you are born down the line this veil descends with a doorway that allows you to see what needs to be seen regarding the lore/law and Nungeena-tya, about the future and about people. How many of you have a small child who plays a lot of the time with what we now call an imaginary friend. They share their food, toys and sometimes everything with this 'friend'. Then one day when they are four or five years old they don't mention their friend again or they say their friend has gone away and they are upset. Their veil has descended. Their friend was real but now their ability to communicate with the spirit world has stopped.

Wanai: from twelve to fifteen years old to between twenty-seven and thirty years old

Usually, sometime between about twelve and fifteen years of age, a young male spills seed and a young female menstruates for the first time. This is a vital time because they then become a wanai.

You are a wanai — an adolescent — from around fifteen to about thirty years old. So as a young female wanai — a dubai — you have about fifteen years of adolescence, depending on when you started to spill seed (ovulate) and menstruate. Young males are wanais from when they spill seed (ejaculate) until they do their final initiation somewhere between twenty-seven and thirty years old. Under the lore/law the Creator decides when you start to spill seed and so effectively when you become a male or a female. Once you spill seed you are able to reproduce and learn the lore/law.

As soon as your seed spills, it goes down into Nungeena-tya and she recognises you, her daughter. She is only able to do this because shortly after your birth, during your Birthing Ceremony, the placenta, with your Miwi print (the map of your spiritual journey), was buried in her. Nungeena-tya now takes your Miwi and guides you as you start your journey.[21] Your grandmothers, aunties and mother have made their commitments to your journey at the Birthing Ceremony so you have a 'bank' of support — with lots of women from whom you can seek advice and guidance and who can teach you the lore/law.[22]

Now you do your wanai ceremony and start developing into an adult and learning the lore/law. You'll make mistakes but because you're a wanai you don't come under the lore/law — the full consequences of your action according to the lore/law. Traditionally your wanai years allow you the space to grow without regrets. During this time you are learning your responsibilities; you're learning right from wrong. You'll make many mistakes at this age, because you've got a pocketful of passion burning a hole. You're passionate about cooking, about clothes and about the boy next door. You're passionate about causes and you want to get placards and rage down the street saying, 'Justice for all!' We make decisions from passion and sometimes our passions get us into trouble.

In traditional society wanais learn from the elders; important teachings on dignity start during these years. The teachings are given at the time they are needed and when they will have the most meaning. For example, say the wanais and the older women have gone out hunting and gathering. A wanai finds a big patch of yams and she calls out, 'These are mine, these are mine!' Everyone can see that it's a big patch of yams — enough for everybody. There's far more than her family could eat. So the elder, the teacher, will stop them there and then and tell them the story of 'how greed was born'. Because her peers are around there is a sense of shame to be brought to task with the teaching so she is more likely to remember what she's been taught and develop a sense of humility. It's not that the elder has deliberately set out to shame her — the shame has arisen from her self-realisation. This is how the wanais learn the teachings about the emotions — learning to be boss of self. In our wanai years we get our most valuable lessons. It's not that we're going to be a 'goody two shoes' later on. These lessons give us a deeper understanding and more compassion for the generation coming behind us.

Migai or Yinarr: from thirty to fifty years old

When you reach thirty, in traditional society, you are now a woman — a migai. There is a ceremony and then you start life again with a clean slate. Under the lore/law, whatever you did before you were thirty cannot be spoken of or held against you in any way. It's against the lore/law. Everything you've ever done while you were a boori and a wanai becomes non-existent spiritually. Unfortunately, many women today have not grown up understanding that their wanai years were a time when it was OK to make mistakes so instead they carry guilt and shame about what they did. This guilt and shame can spiritually cripple us. What we need to do is to try to accept our past mistakes and grow wiser. We can ask ourselves, 'I have done this and what have I learnt?' Regrets can be absolutely useless — excuses to stay stuck and whip ourselves. Give yourself permission to wipe the slate clean. Look in the mirror and say, 'Lovely, gorgeous one, you have been freed from anything you've done prior to thirty.'

Once you're thirty, passion gets married to reason and suddenly you are seeing the world differently. You've still got the passion but reason is there to balance it out, so you become more responsible. This is when you really start to live your Women's Teachings, and now you come under the lore/law. Women become more deeply involved in exploring their essence from forty to fifty years old. At fifty a woman becomes an elder, a senior woman and she begins to share the teaching stories with the wanais. As Memees they will have parenting roles and be involved in the birthing ceremonies.

Memee: once you're a grandmother, or from fifty years old until you die

Traditionally, my friends, this is the 'pavlova' part of life. This is where you come into your true power essence; this is what you have worked so hard for all your life. All your sacrifices are now rewarded. Now you can get away with 'blue murder'. In our society, you don't get what we call 'deadly' until you hit fifty, and then you just get 'deadlier'. When you reach seventy you're at the stage of 'you're so cool you sweat frost'.

We Memees only have to look towards a teapot for a cup of tea to appear in our hand; we only need to frown or purse our lips to make someone drop, cringe and do our bidding. Even now in our society, with so much that is dysfunctional happening, if we turn up somewhere and there is no free seat — and it doesn't matter who's sitting on a seat — without a word said someone will just glance around and then they can't rise fast enough to free a seat for us.

Memees have the big responsibility of showing absolute fairness and wisdom even where it involves their blood kin against non-blood strangers. We are entrusted with decisions about punishment and about distributing children — and we have to treat all as if you gave birth to them. We call everyone 'lovely' because we forget their names and that's all right. The younger women tolerate our snide remarks about men's naughty parts, when we are doing 'women's business'. Within our society we are respected and held in high regard. It has often taken incredible hardships to allow us to hold the wisdom of the teachings. We have arrived home to a place worthy.

Chapter 8

THE JOURNEY — INTIMACY WITH OUR OPPONENTS

Remember that under the lore/law, women are the community developers. We have the hearth — the fire, the home. We give birth and feed our children. Females are the nurturers — ruled by the emotions. We are our children's first teachers and the first teaching is about trust. Women's teachings are about being women and our responsibility to ourselves, our family and our community. It's about how we want to see Nungeena-tya, our eternal mother, in another 100 years, how we want to see our great-grandchildren and our great-great grandchildren. So we were created and born to this role — call it our test toward transcending. We start from here — this is who we are on our journey.

And remember too, that from a traditional point of view, we come to this teaching place — Nungeena-tya — for two things, all truth and all knowledge. We aim to be like Biami, our Creator, who is all truth and all knowledge — that's our goal. Oneness is how we describe it. The Oneness in which we honour everything for its place in Creation, for its differences and for what all of us can offer and give back to each other so we can come together, fitting so perfectly that we are One.

Because our Creator is wise, we seek wisdom. And to find this wisdom we need an intimate relationship with all the emotions. Until we have this intimacy they are our opponents. Let us call 'all truth' pure compassion. So compassion is our ultimate goal. It's the getting of compassion and the getting of wisdom. Compassion embodies intimacy with all the emotions and when it blossoms you just know you have totally embraced them. The old women say the spirit becomes incredibly still when this place is reached.

Too much anger burns you up and you can drown in too much compassion. Compassion has to be balanced with passion. With total compassion it's easy for someone to sit in a room and do nothing about

under the quandong tree

changing anything in the world. They need passion to walk their talk. The emotions get disguised and someone can just have pity on the whole world — this is not compassion. You need passion, and passion needs to marry reason so you can discern. Having passion gives you the power to forever explore and grow your compassion.

When passion is married to reason you have the ability to grow true compassion and distinguish it from pity. In this world today I know some great teachers, some of whom are well known, and say they have compassion for the world and individuals but they do nothing when they could do something. For example, a leader could know that some of his senior clever people are abusing their powers to seduce young women. A person brings this to the leader's attention and he says that he has compassion for the lost men and the young women — lost in the sea of suffering. If this leader has balanced passion with compassion he can change things — he can take up a stick and tell his clever men to do the right thing and lead by example, thereby showing their behaviour to be wrong. If you don't try to bring about justice with your compassion you just pity the pitiful. You need to stop blowing smoke up your own arse and do something. It's called compassionate justice — it's upholding the lore/law.

We come back, life after life after life, to journey and receive the teachings that will give us an intimate relationship with our essences — our feelings and emotions. The body does not have a lot of value but we need it in order to develop this relationship because only when we know our emotions intimately will they never control us; we'll control them.

Our journey is our interactions with ants, birds, trees, sentinels — all of Creation — the Oneness. We choose our teachings before we are born, and then we are plugged into the right energy grids when we are born. The guardians of those songlines and Dreaming tracks interact through our spirit guides. We also absorb the essences of the songlines through our feet to our Miwis. The essences of the Creator beings are alive and strong in every rock, bend and curve in the earth. They are there. Our Miwis absorb them like a blotter absorbing ink — it's our knowing.

A feeling is a reaction to an emotion. How do you react to something? Do you laugh, cry, come forward and attack? Or do you run? However you react, it is a response to a trigger and then you have to discern. Is this feeling of fear, anger, hate or some other opponent making me respond like this?

Look at your emotions as if they're plants that you're growing. Suppose someone tells you that if you dig a hole and put a seed in it a plant will grow. So then you dig a rough hole, don't water it and a plant sort of grows — but it's stunted. So you go to this wise (about plants) person and you say, 'It didn't work; it didn't grow properly.'

The wise person replies, 'When there was no rain did you water it?'

'No,' you reply. So you start to water it and the plant gets stronger but it's still very small. Then you ask, 'Why is my plant so small?'

The wise person replies, 'Have you used your compost to feed and mulch it?'

'No,' you say. And back you go to get your compost around the plant but you put too much, too close to the stem and a fungus starts to grow and weaken the plant. And so the process goes on. For a plant to flourish you have to understand the plant and what will make it grow and produce and what will harm it.

Your emotions could have become weeds — sending out their suckers and completely entangling your house. If there are weeds, then how will you control or destroy them? Dig them out, pour boiling water over them, or use poison? In the same way no-one can show you exactly how to deal with your opponents. Everyone is different. And when you are little you can't deal with them very well at all.

A good way to understand this intimacy that we need to develop is to imagine a man was lying asleep in the desert when a snake crawled into his bedding. It was a deadly poisonous snake. He awoke and was terrified; he was in the middle of nowhere. If he had reacted from fear and run for his life the snake would have reacted and bitten him. So he had to lie with his fear until the snake up and slithered away. Then he realised he was more intimate with fear — he only feared 'fear'.

In January 2007 there was an abalone diver who was swallowed by a shark. He understood fear so well that he knew if he allowed his fear to overtake him the shark would take his life so he stayed with the fear — became more intimate with it and rose above it. He reached out of the shark's mouth with his arm holding his knife and stabbed the shark in its eye, causing the white pointer to release him. The diver lived and said from his hospital bed, 'I have never felt such fear.' But he also said that he would be going back in the water because now he truly understood fear. If you are completely intimate with an emotion, only then will you be able to rise above it and see it for what it is — only an 'emotion', an opponent that can be beaten.

When I was a child I learnt about the Christian commandments — thou shalt not kill, thou shalt not steal, thou shalt not lie and thou shalt not commit adultery. In my culture the lore/law is that we must have an intimate relationship with all of the emotions. For the getting of wisdom the emotions are our opponents and we must master them. Our emotions control us. Fear controls us — it paralyses us; lust controls us; ego destroys and leads us astray, leads us off our path. Then there's pride — it's no good. Vanity and intolerance — these are also no good.

We are born with the essence of anger and compassion but we are born into fear. It greets us as we come out of the birth canal. No wonder we battle with it for the rest of lives. One minute you're swimming warm, weightless and safe, and the next minute you're catapulted into glaring lights, metal and hard cold surfaces. Then someone shoves a suction tube down your throat and slaps you to breathe but meanwhile is wrapping you so tightly you can't. In this day and age it is more like being born into terror, with needles being shoved into you as well.

Your life's journey is only a day in the life of your Miwi. So it's like waking up with this big monster attacking you. You're constantly on guard and have no trust. Your Miwi can't speak from the fright. Last time you were born there were probably no masked faces staring at you and it was completely different. So we come in shell-shocked. Where are the soothing strokes and touches? Who is saying, 'I know this has been scary but you're safe now?' You are not offered food or a drink but are taken away from your mother. You're thirsty and terrified but you're chucked aside while the one who just gave birth to you rests.

When we are too afraid to look for comfort at birth the experience can set the pattern for the rest of our lives — abandonment right up front. We are not left with the cognitive memory, because we were so young. But we are left with the emotional memory, which is much harder to process.

This is the start of our day then and we have to get ourselves together enough — get our arse into gear — to get on with life so we can complete our learning tasks. Once upon a time, traditionally when babies were born they were constantly held, going from one pair of strong arms to another, for eight months.[23] In the day in the life of the Miwi this was enough to ease them from their fright and then their Miwis connected more easily to their journeys' maps.[24]

Remember, we are born with the essence of compassion and anger, inherited from the Rainbow Serpent, the first born, and these two emotions are linked up with all the others. There are about eighteen of these emotions that the traditional teachings are about: compassion, anger, ego, vanity, tolerance, patience, fear, greed, envy, love, acceptance, hope, passion, resentment, shame, jealousy, empathy and humility.

You will have noticed that 'love' and other emotions that we think of as 'good' are included in this list and perhaps you're surprised. In order to become whole, spiritually whole, and to graduate from this teaching place and ascend to the Rivers of the Dreaming, and then on to other islands in the Rivers of the Dreaming we must have an intimate relationship with all of these emotions. Remember then they will no longer control us — and we all know how 'love' can control us.

Our emotions are all opponents that we struggle with everyday and we need to know them and how they influence our behaviour. Emotions control us when we don't know them well enough. So in this way we allow them to control us. They can appear and challenge you at any time, often when you least expect it and when you are your most vulnerable. Opponents often disguise themselves; for example, fear will often take on anger's cloak to confuse you.

It is only when you know these opponents intimately that you can immediately recognise them and they can no longer control the way

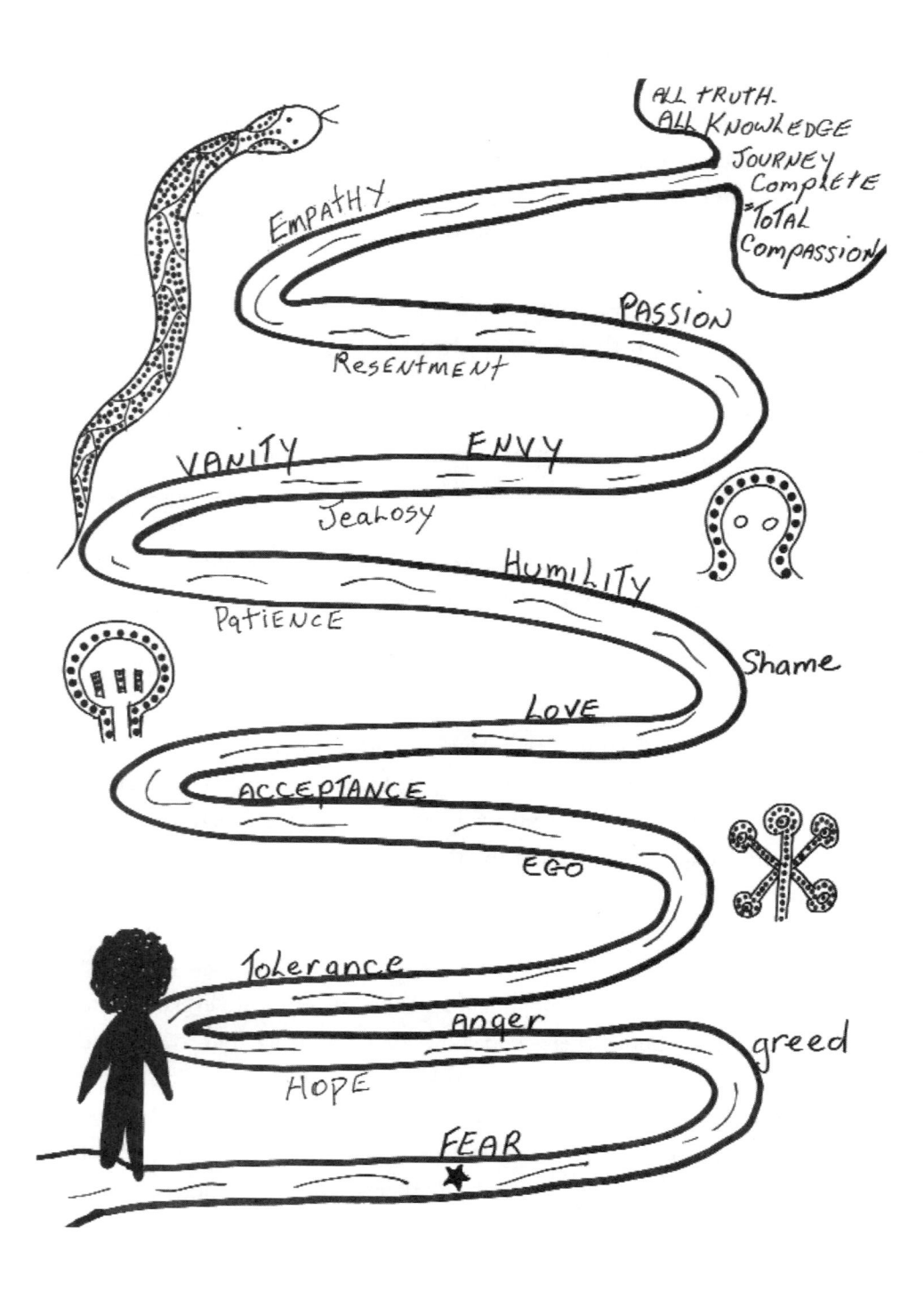

Illustration 12. *The Journey and Our Opponents.*

122

you walk your journey. Once we really know an emotion we feel it welling up and we think, 'Yes, it's OK to feel this way' instead of mindlessly shooting off our mouths and going somewhere else with it. By understanding and seeing this in ourselves at that moment, we also start to recognise this in others. This helps us not to take personally others' opponents because they too are struggling. We develop a higher level of tolerance. We begin to realise that it's OK to feel all of these things because we're all perfectly imperfect.

Now I've chosen to come back this lifetime to learn about tolerance and acceptance. Someone else may have come back to learn about greed, forgiveness or unconditional love. But don't think that because I've written this book and am able to pass on these teachings I've accomplished all these. Think again. Ask my children, my siblings and my friends. I've had my foot in my mouth so many times all my teeth are kicked out and now I have to wear dentures. These teachings are about how we should strive to live under the lore/law and it's a constant, everyday struggle. That's why there is so little wisdom around.

We can't learn about all the emotions in five minutes. It can take a long, long time; maybe many lifetimes. So, suppose as in *Illustration 12*, I get to the star and suddenly become gut wrenchingly afraid and cannot take another step. I'm waylaid and lost in my fear. All these forces are against us and can pull us off our track and our journey, all the time. So perhaps in this lifetime I'll get no further than fear. Then next lifetime I will come and try again to finish learning about acceptance.

In traditional culture, when you're little you learn about your songlines and the emotions connected with those songlines.[25] For example, if you had the she-oak songline influencing you, you would be learning to be careful with your temper (anger) and how to control you temper. The teaching stories are told over and over and over again. We teach our children about love and how to walk a fulfilling journey. From a traditional aspect it's OK to tell your children that it can take many, many lifetimes to learn one lesson.

How to Become Intimate

If you came to me and said 'I want to learn about tolerance' or 'I want to learn about love' or 'I want to learn about acceptance' the first thing I'd do would be to give you a lemon, or an avocado, or an orange, or an apple. And I'd say, 'Tell me its story. Tell me the story of this lemon. Go away and come back when you can tell me the story of this lemon.'

How did the lemon get here? Feel the texture of the lemon. How much of the lemon is palatable? How much of it is bitter? How much can you consume? What part of it can't you consume? What about the lemon tree? Who picked the lemon? What was she feeling at the time she picked the lemon? Was she suffering? Was she impoverished? Was she picking it because she was on holidays? Was it a female or a male who picked the lemon? Who watered the tree? Who fed the tree? What about the storms that hit the tree and the droughts that hit the tree? What about the suffering of the tree? How did the tree become strong? It's not just a lemon, is it? It has a story.

To fully understand or become intimate with something is to know its story. So you could go to your sitting place and really look at the lemon and think about how to understand its story. It's good to practise on fruits and to become intimate with their stories — you'll feel safe because they are unlikely to trigger your opponents. Everything has a story and everything has a teaching.

When you have become confident with fruit you can go to your sitting place and start to give yourself time to really look at different emotions. First you need to let go of all the garbage. The garbage is what we bring with us when we are looking at an 'issue' in our lives. Every one of us feels anger and, rather than accept 'I am angry' we repeat a poopy pot cycle. We carry this little pack on our back — our poopy pot. It's almost like a little spiritual backpack. When we get angry instead of taking responsibility and dealing with it we shove it into our backpack. Then we get resentful that we're angry and that goes in too. Then we become frustrated that we're resentful and we get angry again, and into the poopy pot those feelings go. We carry it around until it starts to drag and then we have to empty it.

This is an example of what are you are likely to do. One morning you get up and go into the bathroom and see the towels wet on the floor. 'Shit!' There's resentment — and into your poopy pot it goes. Then you leave home and get in the traffic and you're held up because 'those Chinese' are stalled at the lights. Frustration — and in it goes. At work the boss says, 'Where's that memo I asked you to send yesterday?' You reply, 'You didn't ask me to send a memo.' 'Yes, I certainly did. Now do it!' You think, 'You shithead!' Rage — in it goes too. All of these emotions are anger, dressed up in different little outfits, coming together in this fashion parade heading towards your little poopy pot. So you are filling and filling it up.

Then you go home and the love of your life walks in the door and says, 'Can I have my blue shirt? I'm going out tonight, luv.' Sweetie's blue shirt is still in the effing ironing basket. You didn't iron yesterday because you were too pissed off with the kids leaving their dirty clothes in the stairwell. So you're thinking, 'I've got to do this now and still got all that to do, and now my mother's calling me on the phone and I've got to go over there. Poor me! I'm just everyone's bloody slave.'

'Your love' asks again, innocently enough, 'Have you seen my shirt?' It's a reasonable question but you lift the lid off your poopy pot and dump. You storm over to the ironing basket, grab the shirt and hurl it at him saying, 'Lift your fat arse and iron your own effing shirt, you lazy bastard!' Done, and then you sigh. For a moment you feel so good. You walk around looking at this poor shredded creature. GUILT! Guilt and more guilt starts to fill your poopy pot all over again. Later you think, 'Why should I feel guilty?' Resentment — in it goes. Then you think, 'Why can't I do something about this resentment?' Frustration goes in. It's anger dressing up again and looking in the mirror and saying, 'How wonderful I am. I'm in control.'

A few minutes later the kids come and ask, 'Can we go to McDonald's for dinner?' Now you reckon it's the ravages of hell to have to eat in McDonald's. So you scream back, 'Over my dead body! I brought you into this world and I can take you out!' Now you've dumped on your little cringing kids. Then you become saintly, 'I did that for your own good! If I didn't teach you, who would? It makes you

under the quandong tree

grow.' That's justification, we can justify it all in a few split seconds and then we start all over again, filling up the poopy pots once more.

We need to deal with our pots. That's part of spiritually growing. Remember: you are born boss of self, you walk your journey boss of self, and you die boss of self. You can just bury your poopy pot. You can just say 'I am really angry' and allow yourself to be really angry without acting it out or dressing it up. A good way to bury your poopy pot is the way you clean your Miwi.[26] You'll feel so good if every time you have a good cry you think, 'All I've done is buried my pot and I haven't wanted to kill or hurt anybody.' Isn't it a lovely way to bury your poop? It's just the best way. We don't want to send our poopy pots out into the Universe and 1000 years from now have them come right back and dump on our heads. It's about self, it's about changing your self. Then you think clearly and you look at things more clearly.

It starts with your intent. Even if it doesn't come out the way you wanted, what's important is the purity of your intention because that's your responsibility. For example, you have come to sit and look at your anger, to become intimate with anger. But you hear this little voice called 'ego' saying, 'I would never get angry if it wasn't for that bitch next door stirring me up, the kids dropping their dirty clothes all over the bedroom floors, the shopkeeper selling me shitty fruit, or that arsehole cutting me off in traffic.' See what an angel you are. What a little saint! You would never get angry if it wasn't for all these rotten people. So who is responsible for what you think and feel? Did you say you? Who is responsible for what you do? Gosh, that must be you too. This is the garbage we need to put aside so we can accept that we get angry and selfish. It's time to take responsibility for our shit — to sit down and grow ourselves up.

Very few people can sit in a place and actually look in and touch their own Miwi but by doing this we are really coming back to self and beginning to understand self. Pick one emotion and look at it. You might choose 'forgiveness'. Then take three or four examples of forgiveness, especially in relation to your partner with his doodle[27], his rampaging you know what, and look into yourself. Ask yourself questions like, 'How tolerant am I? How forgiving am I?' Slowly let go of the things that don't matter like, 'I don't really love you. I'm not going to apologise first for screaming and swearing at you. It wasn't my fault. I didn't start it you did', because this is our ego speaking. We don't look at ourselves enough and we need to. Remember you're not responsible for the journeys of your partner, your children or anybody else; you're only responsible for your own.

As you continue to sit looking at your opponents you are likely to start allowing yourself to understand that we are all perfectly imperfect — that we make mistakes and we're human. And it's OK to be imperfect. Don't beat yourself up for something you did yesterday; yesterday's gone. If you were meant to walk backwards your feet would be turned the other way. As you start to understand yourself, you'll begin to have an understanding of humanity, from a centred place. Because you'll be able to understand others you'll be more tolerant so that you won't jump in and say, 'You bloody great sook, you greedy pig, you vain thing, or you fucking bastard.'

We don't want an entire planet of spiritual eunuchs who are spiritually lost. So start with understanding one thing at a time and it will help you clear your mind and slowly make progress on your journey to compassion.

Teaching Story on Love — How the Waratah Became Red

A long time ago in the Dreaming, before the first War of the Dreaming, Biami said to all in the forest, 'Everything that you need in this life and for always, is within the forest.' Then Biami warned all the small birds, 'Never rise above the canopy of the forest, because the hawk and the eagle go there and they are birds of prey so you will be in danger. You have everything you need within the forest.'

For a long time life went on and then these two little brown birds fell in love. Back then, like today, most birds partnered for life, and one of the teachings in this story is to teach children to honour and respect their life partner.

So the two little love birds decided to build a nest together. The female would fly one way and find a twig and the male would fly another way and bring back a strand and they would weave them into the nest. Then they would nuzzle beaks; they loved each other very much. Finally the nest was almost complete. Now the male always fixes the last strand to secure the nest. So off he went to get the last strand while she went off to get feathers to soften the nest for her eggs.

When the little female returned to the nest, her mate wasn't there. She waited and waited but there was no sign of him. She started to panic. She flew here and flew there, she called and called but he still never came. Remember, she was in love. She was so concerned about him she didn't think about herself. Where could he be? Something must have happened to him.' Finally she decided to fly above the canopy of trees to see where he was as that was the only way she could get a clearer view.

She flew up and up, where she had never flown before, looking, looking and looking for her mate. And she knew the danger but she loved her partner. She looked down one way, and right down the other way, and still couldn't see him. Finally, way off in the distance, she could see him flying towards the nest. Breathing a sigh of relief, she started to descend to the forest floor. As she did, she felt the talons of the hawk pierce her chest. Mortally wounded, she struggled free from the grip of the hawk and fluttered to the forest floor, landing on a white waratah. She was so weak she hopped from waratah to waratah, with her life bleeding away. Finally, just as her partner arrived back, she reached the nest and died.

Her mate wailed and wailed and wailed his song of sorrow. And Biami looked down and was saddened by this. And He came down and said with great compassion, 'I warned you all never to fly above the canopy of the forest. Everything you needed was in the forest. Your partner knew the lore/law and she broke it. But she loved so deeply that no sacrifice was too great and she made the sacrifice of her life for love. The intent within her heart was pure and for this she will be rewarded. To honour her great sacrifice for love, all birds of your kind, from this time and for evermore, will have a blood-stained breast to remind the world of her sacrifice. The female's breast will be redder than the male's breast and the waratahs will forever be stained with her blood to remind the world and all that come after that love in its pure form means sacrifice.'

Now back in the Dreamtime the waratahs were all white, snow white. All along the forest floor grew the most magnificent waratahs you have ever seen. But now all these waratahs became red. Go out into the forest, hold a waratah, but don't break it off. Bend the branch down very gently and put your finger inside the flower and turn it and pull it out. To this day your finger will be stained with the blood of that little bird.

Now the teaching in this story is that to love means making sacrifices. Don't ever think loving somebody or being loved by somebody means that it's all your way; that you are entitled, without giving, to have someone to love you. Love comes with giving. If you think that you are going to love somebody, be prepared, because being 'in love' and loving means making sacrifices; the purest form of unconditional love means making sacrifices. Today this is something we're not so prepared to do any more. Unconditional love is 'loving no matter what'.

Today we are not teaching our children about love and sacrifice. We almost have an entire planet of up-and-coming opthalmologists — 'I' specialists — saying 'me, me, me, me'. Usually both parents work hard all week and on the weekends their children will demand to go to a birthday party, a sleepover, or to their friends for PlayStation and computer games — demand, demand, me, me. And usually what the parents today do is 'roll over' and their excuse is 'I just want peace'. No, you don't! You just want to escape somewhere and that's not true peace. We need to look at how and why we are failing ourselves and our children. We need to teach our children that because they belong to a loving family they have to make sacrifices for each other.

How could we continue the teachings if all the red waratahs disappear from the planet? How could we then be reminded that love means making sacrifices? So it's important to grow waratahs and teach the children right from the start that this is a sacred flower.

Getting to Know Love

In the traditional teachings, to understand love — to become intimate with love — you must be prepared to make sacrifices. That's why we need to remember the story of the red waratah. In my teachings love is not a natural instinct. We weren't born knowing how to love — it is a learned emotion. It's an emotion that's taught and it starts when you are very young. Your parents teach you about love, and then you learn to spread love and belonging out — to the plants and animals and then out further to your whole environment. On it goes, so it's a complete Oneness.

For example a child, even as a tiny baby, will gravitate towards a flower. She'll reach towards it and then Mum goes, 'How lovely, how pretty.' As the child ventures into the garden Mum spreads her own love from the flower out to the beautiful garden and teaches her child how to lovingly care for the growing garden. If Mum has done this well then naturally her child's love will go from the garden to nature, Nungeena-tya and the Oneness of Creation.

Today we're told that love is an instinct and so we believe that a mother will love her baby as soon as she is born. It's not true. Some mothers get this euphoria, from hormones within their bodies, but some mothers look at their baby and think, 'My gosh, what am I going to do about you?' So we need to get to know love.

We say that we 'love' but most of us don't understand 'real love', unconditional love. Almost all the love that's on this planet today has conditions to it. 'I will love you if ... I won't love you unless ... I can only love you when ...' This way of 'loving' is damaging because it's distorted and you justify controlling and manipulating other people in the name of 'love'. There are lots of reasons why we do this, but generally it's because people have grown up to be insecure, fearful, with low self-esteem. Because of their fear and insecurity they need to control and they can mistake this need for love. Then they pass this way of 'loving' on to their partner and then to their children.

For example, we might choose a partner because of certain qualities, we marry them and then we proceed to try to 'change' them. We get the sewing machine out — a little tuck here, a little tuck there, and a button here. We try to create our fantasy and before we know it we're divorced! And we go, 'What went wrong?' We never knew the story of the red waratah, or maybe we had forgotten the teaching about what love means. All sorts of other opponents like greed, fear and ego joined in out of us wanting to create our fantasy or fit in with what we 'think' society expects of us, although much of this is largely through the influence of advertising, TV and Hollywood films.

When we first meet somebody our Miwi connects and it says this is right. Then we ourselves delve into what we want from someone by comparing it to our own level of spiritual integrity — someone we can feel safe with, someone we can be honest with, someone who will be loyal, and to whom we'll be loyal, and someone who is kind. This is our first connection. It starts a deep connection towards a relationship — they're the things we notice. These are important for a life's journey together.

Then our mother says, 'Don't you think he's a bit short?' A week later it's, 'He's very dark. isn't he? He looks Arab. He doesn't have Lebanese blood, does he? You know, dear, those skeletons in the closet? Those people are violent and they do have a strange god.' Then your best friend goes, 'Have you noticed how yellow and crooked his teeth are?' Another friend says, 'His eyes are too close together and you know what they said in *Cosmo* about guys who eyes are close together — they're short tempered and not very intelligent.' These are what I call 'Clayton's friends' — 'friends' when you really don't have any because they are not genuine. Surely you can sense their envy, jealousy and insecurity and yet you insist they're your friends. You listen to them because you don't trust yourself. What your friends think is far more important to you than what your Miwi wants and needs for your journey. Your parents you're stuck with; but friends like that, piss them off and get a dog!

Now for your dad. He's a builder, and he says, 'So your boy's a doctor, you say? Not gay, is he? Not a pussy, is he? Likes football, does he? Just didn't become a doctor to look at women's fannies, did he?' And we haven't even dealt with all your other relatives or your colleagues. By now you are shaking in your boots. So you do one of two things. Out of all these comments, plus input from advertising and TV and movies, you manufacture in your mind the fantasy and off you go looking for it. But will you ever be truly happy? Or you do what your Miwi knows is right for you.

So it's important to undress the emotions around the way we 'love' and see what other emotions are there. This is part of our journey of becoming intimate with the emotions. The saddest thing is that if we don't we are likely to be involved in preventing others — especially our children — from fulfilling their journeys.

I think I would get a different definition of love from every single woman I've met because we live what we perceive to be our own truth. But that doesn't mean to say it's less important than the next person's perceived truth. So our definition of love could be real to us but to someone else it's not real. So it's important to try to understand what we mean by love from as many perspectives as we can.

We need to go to our sitting place and give ourselves time to really look at 'love'. What does loving somebody mean? How deep does it go? Is it real love or is it 'like'? Or is it just 'tolerate'? Is it 'true'? What is 'unconditional love'? Why do you love your husband in a different way to you love your children? You could love somebody very much but are you 'in love'? What's the difference? If your partner wants your body all the time, does this mean he loves you? If you want his body all the time, does this mean you love him? What is lust? What is desire? What is love?

We need to look at our search to receive and give unconditional love, and look at how we go through different illusions and delusions of love. Perhaps sometimes rather than love it's really ego, vanity, fear, or insecurity wearing love's clothes. What do we need to recognise?

If we don't know what love 'is', we can at least start recognising what 'is not' unconditional love. Often we need to look at the way we try to convince ourselves that 'this is love'. Remember we are no more entitled to total love than our partner, our children or our parents.

From a very early age we need to teach our children how to make sacrifices for love and how fulfilling this is. Teach them about unconditional love and tell them the story of the red waratah story again and again. Love means nothing unless we're prepared to give something for it. But if we give to others what we don't really need, is that really giving? We can teach our children that if we love humanity and Nungeena-tya then we're prepared to make sacrifices. It starts in our homes and it starts with little things. First, you teach them how to make sacrifices for other members of the family. For example, you might say, 'Your sister wants to go to this because this is very important to her. So we're not going to the footy this Saturday.' They begin to learn that to love their family they need to make sacrifices, and by enabling them to make sacrifices for the family, they receive the greatest gift that you'll be able to give them because they need to learn about being 'self-less' rather than 'selfish'. You are teaching your children how to have an intimate relationship with love and teaching them how to walk a good journey that will be 'self-full'.

If, on the other hand, you teach your children that 'love' is about having control — 'I will love you if ...' — they grow up knowing and experiencing the withdrawal of your 'love' if they don't do what you want. This feeds your children's fears and they become insecure. This then gives you more control. We do this because of our own fears; this is why we need to become intimate with fear. Fear can consume us. We fear that our children will go off and live great lives and leave us behind. Many, many parents try to live their failed dreams through their children. You've probably heard parents say to their children, 'If only I'd had the opportunity that you've got.'

So we need to look at our fears and also at acceptance. We need to understand our fears to let them go and we need to come to know acceptance so we can accept that we have had our time. We need to get to know gratitude so that we can be grateful for the teachings that we've had. Then, as we learn what love is and we journey towards compassion, we will begin to have empathy for others. Becoming intimate with these emotions is our journey — our Miwi's journey.

Unconditional love is important. The true essence of compassion is important. Walking our talk is very important. The most important is the nurturing of ourselves, our children and then spreading it out to others. Because, when we get to that last second before we leave this life — at the moment of death when our veil lifts — there would be nothing worse than discovering that we had never truly lived.

Teaching Story on Acceptance and Unconditional Love – How the Platypus Came to Be

A long time ago in the Dreaming, down on the Ulladulla River there lived a family of wood ducks, who had a beautiful young daughter. Wood Duck wasn't only beautiful; she was also very obedient, respectful to the Elders, caring and protective of all the little ones. She was just a beautiful person and a beautiful spirit. And a little bit further down the river lived Water

Rat. He was a good, hard-working man, who never hurt anybody, was never spiteful – just a very good man.

One day Water Rat was scurrying over the river, to the little gullies, looking for the most succulent yabbies. He was coming back when he saw, coming down the river, the most beautiful sight he had ever seen in his life. He stood behind a tree and gazed in amazement at this beautiful little Wood Duck swimming down the river. He fell instantly in love. He was absolutely smitten! So he hid there and watched her. Every chance he got he would hide behind his tree and watch the little Wood Duck as she swam.

One day Wood Duck heard a rustle and saw the bushes moving. 'Who's there? Who's in that bush? Come out!' she called. And so, very shyly, the Water Rat stepped out, looked at her and said, 'My name's Water Rat and I live down here.'

She said, 'My name's Wood Duck.'

So every time she came down to that part of the river, Water Rat was there to talk to her. Finally he couldn't hold it any longer and he said to Wood Duck, 'I love you. Will you marry me?'

'How can I marry you? You live in a burrow in the ground and under the water. I live on top of the water. It just can't happen. We are too different.'

And he said, 'Yes, it can. You know I love you.'

'No, it can't,' she replied.

So Water Rat went off to her father and asked, 'Let me marry your daughter.'

'No, you are too different. It can't happen.'

Poor Water Rat just pined and pined and pined. Then one day he heard, 'Help! Help!' He went down to the river and there was Old Man Wood Duck, with his leg caught in the root of a tree that was hanging in the water. His leg was broken.

'Help me! Help me!' cried out Old Man Wood Duck. 'I can't untangle myself and I'll die!'

Water Rat said, 'If you let me marry your daughter, I will help you.'

'I can't do that. It's against the lore/law. You're Water Rat and she's Wood Duck. I just can't do that.'

So Water Rat went away saying, 'Well then, I'll leave you there.'

But he was a good man and he couldn't leave it like that. So he came back and said, 'Let your daughter come and live in my burrow for a few months and see.'

And Old Man Wood Duck agreed. So Water Rat set him free from the root of the tree and Old Man Wood Duck went to his daughter and said, 'Go with Water Rat.'

So, obediently, off she went with Water Rat.

Water Rat had beautiful flower petals covering the bottom of his burrow under the bank of the river and he gave Wood Duck the most beautiful succulent yabbies; he just doted on her. But no matter what he did, she became more and more withdrawn, and sicker and sicker. One day he said to her, 'What's wrong? I bring you the most beautiful flowers and the most succulent yabbies. And you know how much I love you. Why aren't you happy?'

She said, 'Because I don't belong here. I am a Wood Duck. I belong on top of the water, out in the open. I don't belong here, in a burrow.'

And so she started to pine away and began to die.

Water Rat had to go away and think about how much he loved her? Did he love her enough to let her go free and live? He decided that he did, so he went back to the burrow and said, 'You are free. You can go.'

With that she went back to her family.

One day her father looked over and, in among the bullrushes, there was his daughter, just sitting, limp and forlorn. He went over and said, 'What's the matter with you, my daughter? What is wrong?'

And she said, 'I love Water Rat. I love him and I don't know how we can be together.'

Her father thought, 'Here's Water Rat, he's a good man of honour. Here's my daughter who's always been an obedient respectful daughter, always made sacrifices and never spoken back — two very good people. Why can't they be together?' So Old Man Wood Duck went to the top of Goolooga, the sacred mountain, and he swung his bullroarer and called on Biami in the Rivers of the Dreaming. And Biami came and Old Man Wood Duck asked Him, 'Biami, I want you to allow Wood Duck and Water Rat to marry and be happy. Look into their hearts and see how pure their love is. My daughter is a good daughter. She is respectful and obedient, and always cares for the younger ones. And Water Rat is a good man, a hard-working man of honour.'

Biami sat and thought about it. Then He called all the tribes together and He said that because Water Rat and Wood Duck's love was so pure — it was without selfishness — He would allow these two to marry even though they were so different. He would notify the world.

Of course Wood Duck still could not live underground in the burrow and Water Rat couldn't float on top of the water. It just couldn't be. What would become of their babies? Their babies would lay eggs like Wood Duck, feed their young on milk and live in a burrow like Water Rat, have fur like Water Rat, but have a beak and paddle feet like Wood Duck. And so Unconditional Love was born and the Platypus came to be.

The teaching is that it doesn't matter how different you are or what country you come from, if your love is true enough then you should be together. The story of the platypus is about unconditional love and unconditional acceptance of difference.

Getting to Know Tolerance

In order to confuse, your emotions tend to disguise themselves so when you start to look at tolerance you'll see that it can often be wrapped up in another emotion. This is why you need to go to your sitting place and see if you can take the layers off.

What is this intolerance? Where is it coming from? Is it this? Is it that? Is it fear? Is it anger? Often bigotry is just fear. Tolerance can dress up in all sorts of different ways and it likes to sit in intolerance's chair. They steal each other's chairs; they steal each other's clothes; they steal each other's glasses, until you really are confused.

You can spend forever learning about tolerance — learning about the faces of tolerance, the shape of tolerance — and about intolerance, the other side of tolerance. That's why becoming intimate with all the emotions doesn't happen in one lifetime.

People say to me, 'Oh tolerance, I've got that down pat. I'm a really tolerant person. I'm calm, I meditate, and I honour all creatures. I'm really, really tolerant.' Someone, let's call her Jenny, can say all that and then just ten minutes later she's driving down the freeway in her car, looking at the time and thinking, 'Oh shit, I should have been there ten minutes ago.' Rmm rmm rmm, she puts her foot down hard on the accelerator. That's impatience. Patience has gone feral and so it becomes impatience. Now it becomes dangerous. Jenny doesn't have patience down pat. Then just as she comes up to a set of lights, a woman driver cuts right in front of her and puts on the blinker to turn right but Jenny wants to go straight ahead. So she's got intolerance in her ear saying, 'She did that just to get you mad because she's driving a better car than you, she's younger than you, better looking than you, she thinks she's more important than you.' So does she call up her friend tolerance to drag off his outrageous brother intolerance and leave her alone? Or does she give resentment her other ear? And then intolerance begins to say, 'Let my sister anger sort her out. Don't let her get away with this; roll the window down and scream at her.' So anger starts up: 'Bloody Asians, why didn't they finish you off with the bomb? Then you wouldn't be taking jobs from our children, fish from our oceans and the best houses!' Before Jenny knows it she has hatred sitting next to resentment and intolerance, fuelling the fires, until she is no longer in control, they are. Ten minutes before this same person was saying to me, 'Look, I might have a hard time with greed or envy but I tell you I've got tolerance down pat. I'm very tolerant of all people — all races.' Da, da, da.

Getting to Know Acceptance and Patience

To become intimate with acceptance we need to make time and go to our sitting place, our meditation place, to look at what we find difficult to accept. Every single day of our lives we are learning acceptance. What can we change? What can't we change? How can we start to accept the things we can't change? We become 'worked up' about many of the things we can't change; we can't make the lights turn green, we can't cure that man's road rage, and we can't make our kids eat their green beans. Look at these situations one by one until you reach the place of accepting what you can and can't do.

You'll begin to realise that acceptance has a lot to do with patience. It doesn't matter how desperate you are, you can't make your son get out of the shower, you can't make your wrinkles go away, and you can't make your husband stay romantic. Take time to really look at acceptance and patience. Maybe you start to get to know patience and then anger is there, or perhaps you see ego in there making problems. It takes time and patience to undress the different emotions and often when we undress an opponent the underlying emotion is fear.

Teaching Story on Fear – How Courage Was Born

A long time ago in the Dreaming there were all little geckos and all little lizards in the desert. They lived quite happily. Then one day a warrigul came along – warrigul is a dingo. He was territorial and really, really angry. He wanted all the geckos and lizards' territory. Because he wanted their territory he began to kill them one by one. He would rage and rant and go up and down the hill – and Fear was born.

The lizards were so afraid they wouldn't even come out of their little burrows. They stayed there and died of starvation because of fear.

Warrigul would stand on the hillside and he'd say, 'Come out and fight me if you dare! I am the warrigul and I'll destroy you! I want this place, so go away or I'll eat you!' And it went on and on and on.

Because the little lizards were dying one little gecko said, 'If we stay here and be afraid of him, we'll all die. We can't let him do this to us because this is our home. We have to go out and find food. We'll all die. Our children will die, we'll die. Then we'll no longer be.'

But all the little geckos were saying, 'No, no, no – look how big he is! He's so ferocious! No, no, we can't go out there. He'll kill everybody, he's killed our families. He's killed this one, he's killed that one. No, we're not going out there. No, no, we'd rather stay in here. We can't go out there.' They were paralysed by fear.

However this little gecko was having absolutely none of it. He was the smallest one of the lot. (Even though, in those times, they were much bigger than they are now, so were the warriguls!) This little gecko said, 'I'm having none of this. I'm going to go out and fight him. At least I'll die trying. I'm going to do it! I'm going to go out there.' He knew he was afraid. He was so afraid, but still he said, 'I have to go out there and I have to fight him.'

So he went down to the bush and he was thinking, 'How can I do this? How can I take on this great big creature? How can I do it? How can I do it? I'm too small, I'm too weak, and I don't want to be eaten. I'm nurrigah – I can't fight him. But then he thought again, if I don't do it I'm likely to die anyway and he decided deep in his heart that he would take on the warrigul.

Then he went around in the bush until he found a big long piece of vine growing up a tree; he pulled his tail around and thought, 'I'll have to tie this vine here.' This was in case his courage left him too early and he wouldn't be able to do it because fear had consumed him again. He tied the vine round and round and round his tail and put many big knots in it to keep his fear from driving the courage he'd found out of his body.

The warrigul was sitting on the hillside and he heard a voice, 'I'll fight ya! I'll fight ya!' He couldn't believe his ears when he heard this little gecko saying, 'I'll fight ya. Will you be here at sundown?'

'I'll eat you. I'll destroy you!' shouted Warrigul.

The little gecko's voice echoed from the sandhills. 'I'll be there!'

So come sundown, there's this big, big dingo charging up and down, up and down with his testosterone raging. And there's this little gecko coming along the sandhills, with all the courage he'd built up and he was full on.

Warrigul looked down and the closer the gecko got the more he couldn't believe his eyes. Here was this silly little lizard dragging this big long vine behind his tail — with big knots in it! The warrigul just couldn't believe it and he threw back his head and roared with laughter. As he did, the little gecko saw his only chance and sprang at the warrigul's throat. He sank his teeth right into his jugular vein. Warrigul tossed and tossed and tried to throw this creature off, but little gecko clung on with his teeth. (Geckos don't have teeth anymore because they all broke off in this fight.) Slowly Warrigul began to bleed to death.

As Warrigul was tossing, chucking and throwing, fear again overtook the little gecko, chasing courage from him. His courage fled through his tail, blowing it off, so even the vine couldn't hold it. So here's this little gecko with no tail hanging onto this large warrigul. But, overcoming his fear, he hung on until warrigul fell to the ground and finally died. Warrigul's blood stained the earth and formed the red ochre that became men's lore/law. And so courage was born.

There are a number of teachings in this. One is that nothing is too big to take on. If you want to fight to right a wrong, nothing is too big. It does not matter how small you are and how big and strong your opponents are, if you call on courage you will always find a way to defeat them.

A second teaching is that fear is only the shadow of our self-doubt. It isn't real. It is only a shadow. If you shine light at a shadow, the shadow disappears. All you have to do is go to your sitting place and call on the spirit of the gecko, because the gecko is the one who brought courage into the world. You don't have a tail to drop off, so you won't need a vine. But perhaps you'll need to keep remembering this story so your courage doesn't run away.

Now to this very day, if you see a gecko and pick it up, as soon as his courage leaves him, his tail drops off. For evermore he and all his kind remind us of who brought courage into the world. So next time you see a little gecko and his tail drops off, you know that his courage has left him and he's afraid, so just leave him alone. And don't let your kids pull him and play with him; instead, tell them this story about the little gecko and how he brought courage into the world.

Getting to Know Fear and Courage

Today the opponent that we have to battle with, more than any other, is fear. It's an emotion we don't want to recognise because we dare not face our fears: fear of death, spiritual death, or whatever. We need to understand that until we face fear we will never find courage. We're crippling ourselves from fear. Fear is the opposite side of courage. We no longer need to let fear take control now we know from this teaching story that courage has won and can win out again and again. As with the geckos and lizards, overcoming fear can be crucial for our survival. Courage was born after fear — it consumed fear. Courage consumes fear. In order to find courage we must have an intimate relationship with fear because courage is the opposite of fear. They were both born at the same time.

What we do when we feel fear is we change things. We disguise this fear because fear leaves us vulnerable. Take a raving racist who's totally intolerant of anybody that's different. They could be intolerant not just of race but religion and often someone's sex — they're a big red neck. You wouldn't think they're afraid at all but believe me they are. It's likely to be a case of fear wearing intolerance's clothes and sitting in ignorance's chair.

So you need to look at fear carefully. Sometimes it's easier to look at other people first. Watch people's behaviour — people at work or your neighbours. See if you can uncover fear in their behaviour. Can you recognise what people's fears are? Is it fear of disapproval? Is it a fear of failure? Is it fear of rejection? Look at the way they cope with fear. Are they hiding their fears under other emotions? What emotions are they?

For many of us fear comes from our ego. Our ego says, 'Well, no, you really can't do that. You're incapable.'

Here's a office scenario looking at the way we might behave when fear comes up. You're in a meeting and your boss goes to your colleague, 'Oh, Jill, you've done such wonderful work — great reports and an excellent training package.' And then he asks you, 'Have you finished yours?' You reply that it's coming along but you know you're struggling to get the work done. Jill's already asked you if you'd like a hand with the work. But you turned her down. Now there's fear coming up but you don't acknowledge or deal with it, instead you think, 'Bitch! Boss's little pet! She's deliberately done this to put me down.' Now what has happened? Fear is now wearing the clothes of ego, pride, envy and resentment. It starts to pile on all these disguises and it's a wonder it you don't overheat and die!

Once you begin to recognise some of the ways other people behave around fear then start looking at yourself. We need to know ourselves fully, with all our little bits and pieces — our difficulties, our idiosyncrasies and our little naughty parts. Otherwise we will live in a world of illusion and delusion and our Miwis will get more and more contaminated.

So go to your sitting place and just take a short period of time — like the last seven days — and look at your behaviour and see if you can determine when and how you have experienced fear. When it's cold and unsafe we put on all of these clothes but beneath there is a naked body. So peel off all those emotions to look at how many times the core was fear. This is an opportunity to go into your self, to begin to really know yourself. And we can't know anyone else, not even our partner, until we really begin to know ourselves.

You need to look at how you dress fear up. What clothes do you put on it? How do you act? Look at your motives. Try to recognise fear for what it is and ask yourself if you are being true to yourself and true to the universe. When we are lying to ourselves we can't practise our spirituality. Often we do anything we can, rather than face our fear; we lie, we manipulate. The tragedy is that because we can't face our fears we sometimes destroy not only our own journey but also the journeys of others.

Fear is often wearing another opponent's clothes. So see if you can slowly take off all the layers. Fear might be wearing intolerance's clothes or anger's clothes. You usually find ego is in there too. Look at what has made you react like that. Fear is so often controlling us and we just don't realise — that's why it's so important to become intimate with fear. Remember fear is just an opponent and it's no different from love. It's no different from ego. It's no different from vanity. It's no different from intolerance. But it is a strong opponent; next to ego, perhaps the hardest we will battle.

Instead of using fear to make our children do what we want them to do, we need to find the time to give our children the teachings about listening to their Miwis.[28] At first it might take more time but if we teach them by using fear then they will begin to fear almost everything. When children grow up ingrained with fear, there's so much they can't do. They might say, 'No, I can't go to uni, I might fail' or 'I can't go water skiing, I'll drown' or 'I can't go and climb that mountain, I'll fall and break my neck'. It's like a disease and it spreads out further and further.

We need to watch a habit that we could have of always looking at the negative. For example, if your friend says in a surprised way, 'Are you wearing that?' Straightaway you become paralysed and reply, 'Yeah.' Your fear rises up but you disguise it with self-doubt. 'It doesn't suit me,' you think. 'I'm ugly and too fat. How could I have been so stupid to have chosen this? My friend knows best what suits me.' Immediately you have attacked your self-worth instead of instantly calling on courage, looking your friend in the eye and saying, 'Yes I am! Got a problem with that?' And so we disguise our fears with different emotions. We need to be ever mindful in situations so that we begin to know where different opponents pop up.

All these different opponents once we recognise them then seem to manipulate each other so we don't recognise them again. They try another disguise in order to justify their purpose for being there and controlling us. So our opponents can wear all sorts of different clothes: ego might be wearing love's clothes; insecurity could be wearing love's clothes; fear could be wearing anger's clothes; resentment could be wearing cooperation's clothes. But probably the third biggest opponent for people in the world today is greed. Let's now take a look at greed.

Teaching Story on Greed – The Brolgas and the Pelicans

A long time ago in the Dreaming Biami came down and He took from Himself and He blew out across the land and a waterhole appeared and He said to the pelicans, 'All that you and your kind need are within this waterhole. Everything is here.' And the pelicans graciously accepted it saying, 'Thank you, Biami. We are very grateful, and we will live here in harmony.' Then they went serenely into their waterhole and were content. And this went on for a long time.

Biami then took from Himself and He blew across the land and created another waterhole. And He said to the brolgas, 'And this is for you. Everything that you need is within this waterhole.' So the brolgas accepted what Biami had given to them and off they went.

Time went on and one day a brolga looked up over the reeds at the pelicans and he thought, 'Those pelicans are awfully quiet over there.' And he came back down to the others and said, 'Those pelicans are so quiet. They look too happy. Maybe they've got the best waterhole.' And of course all the other brolgas craned their necks and had a look. And there were the pelicans, serene and gracious.

The more the brolgas saw the pelicans' contentment the more it stirred them up. So they started to build within their minds, this 'unfair thing', this delusion about the pelicans' situation. They built on it, built on it, and built on it, and they started to poison each other's minds, until they were all in a frenzy and rage. Finally they said, 'Biami's been unfair. He gave the pelicans far more than he gave us. They've got the best waterhole. Look at them. They're too quiet! No complaints. Look at them!' And the brolgas decided what to do. 'That waterhole should be ours. We'll take their waterhole.' And they all agreed to take the pelicans' waterhole. And so greed was born.

One morning at dawn, the brolgas picked up their spears and stealthily approached the pelicans' waterhole. They attacked them fiercely, spearing and murdering them and the pelicans' blood flowed into their waterhole.

Some pelicans, mortally wounded fled to the skies. And as these gentle creatures flew away, their life's blood poured back across the Earth.

The pelicans were now dead or gone. The brolgas looked around to see what special things these pelicans had that had made them so serene and gracious. But they realised the pelicans' waterhole was identical to their waterhole. It was the same as theirs — exactly the same. They'd slaughtered for nothing.

Biami looked down and was sickened and saddened by the sight. He was horrified and disgusted. So He descended and sat in judgment. He was very angry and said to the brolgas, 'You and your kind have brought greed into the world and for that you will be punished. You know that war dance that you did before you attacked the pelicans, your kind are condemned to perform that dance throughout eternity, to remind all those who follow of who brought greed into the world.'

The opposite of greed, however, is generosity and there was always a positive side. Biami then looked at the pelicans with compassion for they had done no wrong and said, 'You are such honourable creatures. You didn't fight back or spill any blood.' And He gave the pelicans a waterhole far away from the brolgas. Then He waved His hand across the earth, turning to gold wherever the pelicans' blood had fallen. And He said, 'This is a reward for you. You pelicans will always be known for your grace and serenity. The blood you have spilled will be sought by all for evermore and will be given as a gift to remind the world of the sacrifice you made because of others' greed.'

So the sleeping place of the pelican lies under this country. It's the pelicans' Dreaming place — a mountain of gold. Always remember you can call on the spirit of the pelican for serenity and acceptance for the whole essence of life.

Getting to Know Greed

We're at the stage now on this planet where greed has taken over. We may not think that we are greedy or that we are teaching our children to be greedy, but we are. So we have to look carefully and closely at greed. To become intimate with this emotion of greed we need to understand it from every single aspect: how it works, how it thinks, how it behaves, how it manipulates, how it controls and what disguises it takes.

Sit back and first observe your neighbours or colleagues at work, then work your way back to you and your family. Don't start with your family, because we're biased about them. We look at our family through our hearts and that's not usually a clear view.

Listen to your neighbours and you're likely to hear them saying, 'I must have that fridge ... I must have that lounge ... I must have a new verandah ... I must have a carport ... I must have a shed ... I must have a bigger house.' Do we really need so much? When you start to look closely, most of the time you'll see it's just greed driving people. There can be a difference between greed and buying quality. If you buy something that will last and last, it doesn't steal from your grandchildren. Remember, we don't inherit the earth from our parents, we borrow it from our grandchildren. If we buy something that is good quality that we keep and care for, well and good — it could still be around for our grandchildren's use. But watch out that ego isn't walking hand and hand with greed and saying, 'I want to be better than so and so because I'm more important than them and must have the best.' Look carefully! Is it about impressing others? Has it gone from greed to ego?

Biami said when He created us that we were born with two hands, one to give with and the other to receive with. If somebody has a stroke and they can't use a hand or a limb, what happens to the hand? It shrivels up, it shrinks. Because it's not used it becomes atrophied. How many people in your neighbourhood have composts? People say, 'Oh, they're smelly!' But if you get or make a proper compost and maintain it correctly it won't smell. It will enrich the soil giving back to our mother, Nungeena-tya, rather than just continually taking from her.

Focus on yourself and ask, 'Where am I? Do I have what I need or do I have what I greed?' We all need a roof over our heads; we need food; we need clothes on our back. But we can only wear one shirt at a time.

This is about your spiritual journey. When you come back again, do you want to come back into a toxic environment? You might think, 'Yeah, yeah, you don't know for sure about reincarnation.' But what if reincarnation is correct? What if you do have to come back again? We need to leave something behind and remember, there's only the one teaching place — Nungeena-tya — and she's a mother who's got a lot of babies she's trying to nurture. She can sustain far fewer greedy babies. To be part of the Oneness we need to do our bit.

The lore/law says: 'You take only what you need and not what you greed.' This is the essence of Oneness — by taking what you need you are taking what is rightfully yours. When you take what you greed you are taking at someone else's expense. Then you have set yourself apart or above the rest of Creation. We are all 'no more' and 'no less' than anything else that is created.

Getting to Know Ego

Remember the story about the birth of ego? Ego was born when the golden sunset spiders decided their webs were perfect and started to make them more and more intricate and spread them everywhere. The webs began to suffocate everything. The golden sunset spiders didn't care that everyone was dying under their webs.[29] Ego is a delusion — it's a false sense of self-importance. It's probably one of our most difficult opponents because it has the power to cause our spirits, our Miwis, to lose their consciousness. We battle with ego all the time.

Today we've become so spiritually insecure and disconnected that our egos demand that we seek approval from strangers. The lore/law says: 'One only has to walk this life with dignity. No-one can take dignity away from you — you give it away.' Ain't this the truth, sisters?

So many of us buy into needing approval from neighbours we don't even know. You would have heard people saying, 'No, don't go out like that, what would the neighbours think?' or 'We have to mow the lawn on Saturday so we can't take the kids to the park. Otherwise what will the neighbours think?' or 'We can't have those banners hanging there. What will the neighbours think?' or even 'You can't have all these black, Asian and Indian people running in and out your house. Your neighbours will think it's the Hotel Anybody.'

When you finish your journey you only need to be satisfied with you. I'm at the end of my life and all the people I have impressed and whose approval I have sought do not matter to me. The only people that matter to me are those whom I have loved and those who have loved me. And that's all I want to take with me.

When you're at your sitting place looking carefully at ego ask yourself, 'What is ego dressing up in? Is it fear? What is this fear? Is it fear of not being approved of? Is ego controlling you saying, "You can't do that? You're too stupid."' Ego often tells us we're not good enough. Are ego and greed walking hand and hand? Is ego piggy-backing vanity? It's important to look carefully at how these opponents work together — and then slowly you can separate and understand them more deeply. When you are at ease and completely OK with them they won't control you and you won't have to act them out.

Getting to Know Vanity

Now remember that vanity was born when the giant green ants spent their time looking at their reflections in a pond. Then with their poisonous enzymes they started to kill everything that stood up to them.[30] Most of us know that we are vain. And men are vain too; even animals and trees are vain. But we girls are very familiar with vanity — we know it well.

When someone asks us, 'What are you wearing to the party tonight?' Rather than replying, 'Well, I'm wearing my slacks' or 'I'm wearing my dress', we are more likely to say something like 'I'm wearing my "Laura Ashley". What are you wearing?'

Vanity is just something that we know is there. Why do I go and get my hair dyed? I justify my vanity by saying, 'It sits better and I feel better.'

We should watch vanity very carefully, it can take us over especially when we try to become like a celebrity whom we've seen on television or in a magazine. The danger is we could just become an image, lose all sense of self and lose our path. Vanity is bugeenge and it pollutes our Miwis.

Spend some time looking at other people's behaviour around vanity. Is vanity dressed up as fear? Go to your sitting place and look at vanity. Am I aware of my vanity? Are people around me vain? What emotions dress up in vanity? Does greed walk hand and hand with vanity? Is ego there too? Do I justify my vanity? What am I teaching my children and my friends about vanity?

By doing this we can become more familiar with this emotion of vanity, and although it can continue to cause problems it will be less threatening to us because we know it. That's why we need to look at all our opponents, especially those we aren't so familiar with — like love and anger — and those that affect other people more.

Let's now look at the destination of our journey — the getting of compassion. Compassion embodies intimacy with all the emotions and when it just blossoms you know you have totally embraced them. The old women say the spirit becomes incredibly still when this place is reached.

Teaching Story on Compassion – How the Kangaroo Got Her Pouch

A long time ago in the dreaming, Biami looked down on all of us and shook his head because he saw such greed and selfishness. He was sad. Now Biami is never spiteful or cruel, never, but He can be sad.

'Look at them', He thought. 'I have to go and see just how selfish and greedy they are.'

So He came down and turned himself into an old wombat and sat on the side of the road. Along came a warrigul. 'Please help me,' He said to the warrigul. 'I'm blind and I'm thirsty and I'm hungry, and I need water and food.'

'Grrggh, out of my way, you stupid old thing!' said the warrigul. 'Go on, git!'

Then along came emu and old wombat said, 'Please, please help me. I'm blind and I'm thirsty and I'm hungry. Please help me.'

Now the emu was in a hurry, you know, a big fast hurry. 'GO! Go on! Get out of my way!' said the emu.

One by one the animals came. And one by one they all abused or ignored the wombat. Every one of them was either in a hurry to get to some important place, or had some greed to fulfil, or was just too plain selfish.

Then along came a kangaroo, a mother kangaroo. Kangaroos didn't have pouches then. They carried their babies – that's why kangaroos have hands. They are very adept with their hands.

So this mother kangaroo was carrying her baby and she looked down on old wombat with compassion. 'I am carrying my baby,' she explained. 'So it's hard to guide you unless you hang on to my tail. It will be a very bumpy ride but I know a place of green, green pastures and sweet, sweet water where you'll be safe.'

Biami hung on. I don't think He quite bargained for what He got – but beggars can't be choosers when you're searching, even Biami.

So He hung on to her tail and off they went. She bounced Him all over the place. It's a wonder He didn't have concussion by the time they got there. Well, He might have, I don't know, I haven't met Biami to ask, but I will when I see Him!

The kangaroo took Biami to the green pasture and sweet water. Then, just as she was about to leave, she looked up. Because kangaroos can be very tall, right across the other side of the water, she could see the hunters coming. 'Get down! Get down!' she warned the old wombat. 'The hunters are coming and you're in danger. Stay low and I will lead them away from you.'

She clutched her baby firmly, got the attention of the hunters and then took off. The hunters, holding their spears, yahooed and ran behind her. They wanted meat!

It was a long time later and dark when the kangaroo came back, sobbing and heartbroken. She said to old wombat, 'I've lost my baby. I put her down and now she's lost in the dark. I think the hunters got her.'

Biami was filled with compassion for the sacrifice this stranger had made for Him. He said, 'Lay down now and sleep and in the morning you can look for her.' So the mother kangaroo lay down and cried herself to sleep.

'She needs to be rewarded,' Biami thought. So He went over to a paperbark tree and tore off a big piece of bark.

Just as the sun was rising the mother kangaroo awoke to see Biami laying the piece of bark across her stomach, sealing it to her body and placing her baby in her arms. She looked into the Biami's eyes. 'Biami?' she asked.

'Yes,' he replied. 'I am Biami, and I have tested you. I became the blind wombat because I was testing all Creation for greed and selfishness. You were selfless in your sacrifice for a stranger. You and your kind are now rewarded and will, throughout eternity, have this pouch to carry your babies in. From this day on you and your kind will only ever be able to go forward. So all those who need to move forward from pain or suffering can call on your spirit to take them.'

under the quandong tree

Now every time you see a female kangaroo with her pouch you'll be reminded of the story of Biami. But more importantly is this: whatever your beliefs about a Creator or Great Spirit, you'll just never know where, when or how they will appear. Is it that rat that keeps chewing at the back fence? Or is it that old dog that someone gave you as a puppy that is now chained down the backyard and never given fresh water and daily food or taken for a walk. You never know. It could be that the person sitting right next to you is Biami testing you. When we get up each day it's important to remember that we don't know when or why we'll be tested — or if we'll pass the test.

Part Three

Chapter 9

THE STORY OF THE EIGHT SISTERS

Remember that after creating this teaching place, Nungeena-tya, and because of what happened in the very beginning of Creation,[31] Biami always came back and forth from the Rivers of the Dreaming. He would physically manifest and walk in His Creation. His footprints can be found at Brewarrina and up in Wilpena Pound, and also where He came to look for His son at South West Rocks in the Evans Head area. They're big and there's a sacredness about them.

In the womb of the earth lies sacred water that has never been touched by sunlight and there, beneath the sacred rock, was Biami's sitting place — His sacred cave. He came here to meet with His lore/law people. These were the kadaitchi and wirrloo that carried out and taught his lore/law. He was absolutely the most powerful but they weren't very far behind.

There was always men's lore/law, women's lore/law and our lore/law. That is why it is called men's business, women's business and our business. Partly the reason there was men's business and women's business was because Biami insisted that each is as important to this planet as the other. Men and women should be validated in their own right and have their teachings and their own collective consciousness, I guess. Why? Because we are very different. In fact, male and female are very different. These days we're trying to make men women and women men and expect them to think like each other. But, believe me, it's not going to work. We're just going to end up with confused kids. So grab your womanhood and say, 'Yes! Yes!'

In the cave there were two power stones or crystals. They were within a vortex that opened a doorway, allowing Biami to move freely between the Rivers of the Dreaming and the physical world. He needed caretakers for His sitting place so He requested that people offer themselves up to be the keepers. Eight sisters offered themselves. They would take care of this most sacred area and protect the two power stones, and Biami trusted only these sisters to guard this sacred area.

There was a pathway down from the sacred rock so Biami would meet in His cave with kadaitchis and wirrloos. They'd say to Him, 'Yes this is happening and this and this.' Once they had filled Him in they would receive more teachings from Him — more lore/laws. He would say, 'You know how this is happening here? Well, now this needs to be done.' Or, 'You need to go and walk with fear. You need to go and walk with courage. You need to go and do this or do that and take people with you.' The Creator was very giving so they always had access to His help and most people very much wanted His wisdom.

Every time Biami came He was revered by those He had created. Anyone who could come up with a planet this good and make us so perfectly imperfect in spite of all that happened, He's got to be deadly! Let's face it, if I could achieve anything near it I'd be wearing a t-shirt that said, 'I'm so cool I sweat frost!' So yes, Biami was revered — and so He should be.

However this kadaitchi lad started to become irritated, really irritated because he thought, 'Every time Biami comes and walks this earth everyone drops everyone else and brings Him the best food from what they've got; they can't do enough for him. But He's just a man like us. That can come and go. Anyway does He really go to the Rivers of the Dreaming and da-da da-da da-da?'

So the lad got quite nurrigah, twisted up with envy, ego, greed and arrogance, all of these festered in him until he became totally rotten — a wirrinun. One day he thought if Biami wasn't around, he could rule the world. Absolutely. Everyone would have to kowtow to him because he was such a powerful Magic Man. So he plotted away: 'If I take those power stones and close the doorway then Biami can't get back. I will have the power because I will have the stones.' To get these crystals the wirrinun decided to kill the sisters. But the fool didn't realise that 'death' had already been born, and he was but a mere mortal.

The Killing of the Seven Sisters

If Biami had been a God that was firm, hard and vengeful, He would have turned this wirrinun into one of the pebbles beneath the sacred rock. But He knew what was going to happen, so He prepared for it.

under the quandong tree 153

He had opened a secret passage out of His cave for the sisters to escape. Everyone else knew of only one entrance, the one that all the clever people came through.

The eight sisters were literally light-blinded because the only illumination in the cave came from a kind of luminous stone. So, with stealth, the wirrinun went down with a fire stick and blinded the sisters. One by one he began to kill them. Seven died fighting to hold him back, giving up their lives for the eighth sister so she could escape with the two crystals.

The Escape of the Eighth Sister

The eighth sister grabbed the power stones and fled through the secret passage, the one that only Biami and the sisters knew. As fear overtook her, in her haste, she dropped one. There was nothing she could do about dropping it because she knew that she was being pursued.

She held onto the other stone tightly and ran and ran and kept on running for most of that day. Biami watched her run and saw the wirrinun pursuing her. But Biami was helpless. So because Uri's (the sun) energy is so powerful He said to her, 'Beat down and slow him down. Become really, really hot and slow him down.' And she did.

The Collapse of the Eighth Sister

Finally the eighth sister fell exhausted to her knees, clutching the crystal to her breast. 'Biami, I can't go any further,' she cried.

There had been enough time for Biami to send energy into Nungeena-tya to take over His power. Nugeena-tya opened to embrace the sister as she fell to the ground, encasing her in a crystal core to protect her. This was, I suppose, what scientists would call a volcanic eruption.

So the eighth sister lies sleeping on a Dreaming track, enclosed within the crystal. To keep her safe, a golden crystal core with every colour of the rainbow formed around her. Biami then said to Uri, 'Every day, kiss the eighth sister with your energy. Send it down to protect her and then send it out along the Dreaming tracks.'

Uri kisses the eighth sister every morning and as the light travels down the crystal core it spreads out along the Dreaming tracks right across this country to the sacred rock with Biami's cave. This energises all the Dreaming tracks throughout this continent every day then feeds out into the songlines, keeping all of Creation strong.

Where the eighth sister sleeps is a place we call Wuuluumbin (Mount Warning) which is at the back of Lismore in northern New South Wales. It was once a volcano. To ensure that no-one can take that crystal from her, every morning the sun touches the top of this mountain first. It is the very first spot on this continent that the dawn reaches. What a way to live — being kissed every morning forever by Uri!

The Wirrinun's Attempt to Duplicate the Power Stone

The wirrinun managed to get only one of the power stones — the one the eighth sister had dropped. This powerful crystal didn't come from this earth; it came from the Rivers of the Dreaming. But the wirrinun thought that he needed two crystals together. If only he could duplicate the one he had he would hold the power and Biami would never get back.

He had heard of a people who were Masters of Crystals, and the wirrinun thought that if he found them, they could duplicate the crystal. So he sailed in his canoe over the ocean. After years and years of searching he found this race of people and their country. They were indeed experts in the creation and making of crystals. So he asked them to duplicate his power stone and, if they agreed, that they would then share the power he would have over the world. He promised them, I think, all sorts of dominion over Creation, rather than simply being the keepers of it. And so they agreed to duplicate the crystal.

What the crystal masters and the wirrinun did not know was that Biami would not allow the crystal to be duplicated. And if you did duplicate the crystal it would set in motion a force that would be like a negative and a positive hitting together. This would create the most massive explosion and bring about your own destruction. So as they duplicated it the entire place blew sky high; the continent imploded and sank to the bottom of the ocean. The people, the wirrinun and the original crystal fell to the bottom of the ocean where they still lie today with the stone still intact, the second key to Biami's doorway.

Wuuluumbin (Mount Warning) Today

It doesn't matter if you're a Catholic, Buddhist, Jewish or whatever, this is our land we are born from, or where we have chosen to be. It's very important that we all get in touch with this belongingness — the part of us that can really honour each other and each other's right to be here. Otherwise we're not going to do any good at all. It doesn't matter what country you come from, what religion you belong to, when you're down and down and down and you've got nowhere, you really need something. Some people go and sit in a church. Often it's got nothing to do with the fact it's a church; it's to do with the Divine Energy and the peace within. So it's the energy that you seek — and the safety and comfort of this energy can be found there in the church.

Similarly this is our land. It was created by the Creator for us and there are energy tracks and resources all over it that we can tap into for soul food. This energy is as rightfully yours as it is mine. There are light lines going all over the place, connecting mountain to mountain to mountain, connecting places where ceremonies are carried out. It's the same as going to a church. It's where you can seek spiritual direction and strength.

Wuuluumbin is a very powerful women's place, very sacred. It's on a positive Dreaming Track and is such a significant area because it is where the eighth sister sleeps, still holding that power stone. Remember, it is the first place the Sun touches this continent each day — and this is to keep this crystal safe from the wirrinun and all those who come after.

If you go to Wuuluumbin there are some things you need to understand. If you go to this mountain at dawn and you have negativity, anger or vengefulness in your heart everything that you feel within your Miwi will be magnified a thousand times. So if you're there with negativity it can increase to such a degree that it could physically kill you, that's how destructive it could become. If you are a seeker and when the Sun first touches this place at dawn you go there with a positive aspiration or dream, that too will be increased a thousandfold. You can achieve anything, especially if your thoughts are for the healing of humanity or developing your contact with Spirit.

If you're at Wuuluumbin at dawn and out of the mist and fog, just as the sun hits, the Spirit of the Rainbow Serpent appears and swirls around you, then you are meant to achieve great things for the healing of humanity. This is a significant event. It means you will be supported. You've got spirits watching and guiding you.

Chapter 10

THE BREAKING OF BIAMI'S STONES

Nungeena-tya, our Earth, moves on different Dreaming tracks. In fact, the whole universe is moving and changing, all the time. Nothing stays still. Nothing stays the same. Your spirit doesn't stay the same. Your body obviously doesn't stay the same. Nothing ever stays the same.

Our solar system is moving on a Dreaming track.[32] It's been on this track for thousands of years. Since Creation it has changed Dreaming tracks many times, and our solar system moves from track to track through Nungeena-tya changing the tilt of her axis, the speed of her rotation and her vibration.

Once we used to walk upon land that was where the ocean is now. In those times the planet was on a different Dreaming track. And as the planet continues to move on different Dreaming tracks the oceans could completely tip again. Do you really believe that this is the only time we have evolved or that we are the only race that has existed? No! No! No! This planet has been going for billions of years. We didn't just evolve; we have come back, back and back again. We are changing because we're evolving spiritually. Remember, we choose to come back and learn about tolerance, acceptance and all our opponents. We come back to learn the lessons we need.

I have explained earlier that we move onto different tracks about every 5000 years.[33] All these tracks are about self-knowledge and self-consciousness. We are now coming out of a Dreaming of physical knowledge and moving into a Dreaming of higher consciousness and awakening.

Dreaming tracks carry the essences of the Creator's divine energy. And because we also have the Creator's essence we have the potential to reveal divine characteristics. While we were dreaming of the physical we lost our way — and so greed, ego and vanity consumed us. So now — and not for the first time — we are the blight of Creation and no longer its keepers. However, many people are coming to understand that we are destroying not only Nungeena-tya but also each other.

It is said in our teachings that it will be humanity who will destroy humanity. I interpret this as meaning that humanity could eventually self-destruct. People say, 'We should make these people do this. We should make the politicians do that. We should make sure they take care of the young people. And why don't they do something about drugs?' But it's up to us. Only we can make a difference, starting from self.

It may be difficult to believe that we are tit-fed people. We were born on the tit and will die on the tit. Everything we consume comes from the Earth, our mother. I don't care who actually prepares or processes what we consume and I don't care about the way we get it to our being. Everything that we take to ourselves is breast milk from Nungeena-tya — and if she dies, we die.

Biami's Stones

Over the last few centuries the Earth's positive Dreaming tracks had started to lose energy and close down because of the destruction to ourselves and to Nungeena-tya. When events of destruction have come from bugeenge intent — through massacres, injustice, wars and extermination — and if these took place on a Dreaming track, then the track would be broken at the place where the destruction occurred. For example, there is a major break at Pine Gap in the Northern Territory where there is a large Dreaming track junction. Tracks join here from many places — the Glasshouse Mountains, Obiri, Wilpena Pound, Wave Rock, Uluru, Kangaroo Valley, Goolooga and Wuuluumbin, to name just a few.

Our spirituality had almost died. You see we were in a spiritual coma. Over the last few hundred years, humanity had, very rapidly, declined into a spiritual lostness or spiritual malnutrition. People were not feeding their spirits but feeding their egos instead. Our Miwis were shutting down and only the computer-mind was working, allowing ego, greed and other opponents to completely take control. Look around you. If you are a woman and not youthful, beautiful and almost skeletal with big tits you have no value. If you're a man without a penis extension, hair implant or waxed body then you won't get a second glance.

We were well on our way to destroying ourselves, humanity and the planet and Biami could not get back to help us as He had before. Remember in the story of the Eight Sisters that the wirrinun, driven by greed, ego and jealousy, destroyed the doorway between the Rivers of the Dreaming and Nungeena-tya.[34] Biami knew all along that this was going to happen.

After the War of the Dreaming, deep within His cave where the first-born was created, Biami left a set of stones with the Sisters. These stones had sacred — very sacred — engravings on them. They could be picked up and, when there was a certain planetary alignment, broken to bring universal divine energy into Nungeena-tya. This would move the solar system onto another Dreaming track in order to heal Nungeena-tya and those living on her.[35] It was not the first time this had happened.

In this way Biami could help with his love, sending it through Nungeena-tya and, by way of our connectedness to her, up through us. Because we were suffering from spiritual lostness, spiritual paralysis and selfishness we had to see just how bad things had become with Nungeena-tya before we could stir ourselves into action. We had to save ourselves this time around and follow the road to the teachings. From out of all of this chaos we had to find the path to save the teaching place.

Biami knew that one day we would need His stones because our greed would get the better of us. Nungeena-tya started to die because we just insisted on 'kill kill', 'rape rape' and 'plunder plunder plunder'. And when she started to die, that was when the stones needed to be broken.

The Decision to Bring Back the Lore/Law and to Break Biami's Stones

In 1987 I knew that some of the clever men in this country were planning big ceremonies. Something vital was going to happen. The following year, 1988, was to be the bicentenary of 200 years of white settlement in Australia and at first I thought it was going to be a massive big black and white war. I thought, 'Oh shit they've got guns and they're going to kill and massacre and there'll be bloodshed.'

I wasn't told first up what the men were about, but during 1987 there was a meeting of all the 'clever people' — the senior people — about 'the return of the lore/law' and the breaking of a certain set of stones. These were the final lore/law stones — or Biami's stones — and they had great significance. Their breaking would impact on the entire solar system. And it turned out that the clever men were doing the big ceremonies to bring back the lore/law.

Biami gave the lore/law men the responsibility to discern whether to invoke this power. They first met in 1985. Then, for a couple of years, circles of both senior men and women grappled with this choice. There was a lot of conflict. Many of the old people said, 'No, if the lore/law is brought back and the stones are broken it will mean that we'll spiral towards destruction. It will escalate the destruction of the planet. Nungeena-tya will die and we'll die with her.' Others said, 'We've got time. We still have time. It's very close but we still have time.' Some were shunning anything to do with the lore/law.

So there was a whole lot of kerfuffle and anxiety. The stones had to be broken at an exact moment in time — with the planets aligned in such a way as to allow a free path for the energy from the Rivers of the Dreaming. Otherwise, we would have had to wait for another seventy to ninety years, which could have been too late to prevent the second War of the Dreaming. So the choice was made and the exact moment was to be 7.30 pm on 7 May 1990.

•••••

About every thirteen decades Nungeena-tya passes more deeply through the war Dreaming track. During this passage she is in danger of being hit by meteorites that are the remnants of the first War of the Dreaming, the bugeenge that Biami turned to stone. The danger period lasts for about two decades. And about every three decades, when the Earth does a wobble on its orbit, the Middle East just touches the war Dreaming track. Once the stones were broken Nungeena-tya would move to another Dreaming track, which would have happened in about another 100 years anyway. But to move earlier would mean that the Earth would move more quickly by many years, through the war Dreaming track.

I had also heard that after the stones were broken, when the time came, the two crystal power stones that had formed Biami's doorway would again come to light.[36] One would rise from the seabed in order to be found. It was only just a couple of years ago there was a volcanic eruption in the ocean somewhere, and as a result of the lava an entirely new island surfaced from the bed of the ocean. I think the crystal is in there. Wuuluumbin would rise up and hand back the other stone. So, this mountain again will part but I can't see it just parting; it may well be on account of an earthquake or, because it's an extinct volcano, there could be a volcanic eruption. Then the two crystals, at some stage, would go back to where they belong in Biami's sacred cave at the bottom of the sacred rock.

I was scared; everybody was scared. I think the whole planet was scared but they didn't know what they were scared about. Perhaps everybody knew that we were on the brink of something. It's not a conscious knowing — it's a spirit knowing, a Miwi knowing. We sense that we have to do something now but we get so confused. We think, 'Oh, it's too big.' But imagine if every single human took good care of only themselves and set about changing only himself or herself. What a glorious planet we'd live on!

So early in 1989, us trainee lowlies were taken in and told that the stones were to be broken at 7.30 pm on 7 May 1990. I knew about the tjuringa and the ogkteringa[37] and I thought they were talking about these, but they told me it was Biami's stones instead. I was given my stone, the one I was to break, but not in my country. Many Indigenous tribes no longer existed so there was no wirrloo or kadaitchi for their country. These lore/law people were dead but right around Australia our people responded by choosing different ones to break the stones in different lore/law countries.

The Breaking and the Opening of the Dreaming Tracks

At that designated time in 1990, 300 stones were broken in Australia and others were broken elsewhere around the world.[38] An incredible vortex opening was created so that Biami could send light through

Nungeena-tya. It then took six years for the Earth's Dreaming tracks to fully open, bringing back the universal energy into Nungeena-tya. It was a slow process because the energy was so great that it could have blown the planet apart.

I had to break my stones in a completely traditional way — but smack bang in the middle of the city. Yeah, I was all painted up — a white ochre face with feathers and naked to the waist! The stones were broken using stone on stone and then dropped. The crack echoed all around. Immediately I turned to leave but three Kooris who had just come out of the pub were in my path. Then I heard these terrible screams. People driving along nearly hit the telephone poles at the traffic lights. That was the last thing I remember until I was back in the car. A police car had pulled up beside me and when I looked at them they just drove off, straight through a red light. So it frightened a few people; they must have thought that the end of the world was coming.

After the stones were broken the decision was made that all women would have access to traditional women's teachings. How can you care for your country — your land, your mother Earth and all living beings — if you are not taught how? How do you know who you are or where to go without guidance? There's an opportunity to awaken your Miwi when you are given the teachings and then you can make your choices. But for every choice there's a consequence — that's life, that's our journey.

From 1990 to 1996 there was an awakening like no other. Those people who had built careers and wealth slowly became aware that there was something far greater that seemed far more important. They began to see the interconnectedness of everything and how important it was, not only for humanity, but all living things. Their Miwis were awakening so they were becoming aware of our purpose of 'Oneness'. They were becoming aware that our planet was dying and the part our greed was playing in this impending death of our mother and realising that if she dies we die with her.

Spiritually these people had been empty but now, all of a sudden, they had woken up. There was something they had to be doing. They were on a search, although for what they often didn't know. They only knew they had to find whatever it was. This was often their first step in their vision quest for spiritual fulfilment.

When someone has been in a coma for a long time and they wake up, the first thing they ask for is a drink of water. 'I'm really thirsty,' they say. The awakening of people's Miwis was like this. They woke up and realised they were needy. Their spiritual lives were wanting; they were thirsty for something, even if they couldn't identify what it was. People realised they were being slaves to society's unrealistic expectations. No matter how much they achieved there was always a higher notch to attain, but towards what? They woke up to realise that their children had grown and gone and they didn't even know them. They woke up as old, old people and knew they had never really lived. It was a kind of emptiness, an emptiness that cannot sustain humanity. They realised they needed to be doing something much deeper than materialism. Status no longer had meaning; projecting an image in society seemed useless.

Millions of people realised, during the six years of the opening of the Dreaming tracks, that it wasn't physical things that fulfilled them, it was discovering the Oneness that gave meaning to everything they did. Then Nungeena-tya had the power to touch these people and say, 'It's time to save the teaching place, to save humanity through healing yourself.'

The Stones for Re-joining and Strengthening the Dreaming Tracks

During the six years from 1990 to 1996, teaching and lore/law stones from all over the world had to be gathered. Some had to be brought back to Australia, others put in different places. In other words, before the solar system shifted to a different Dreaming track some of the stones had to be moved to new parts of the Earth's Dreaming tracks. This would keep the energy in alignment and these stones would then join the light lines together for the new Dreaming track. Different people were chosen for the gathering, moving and placing of the stones. Part of my job was to go and pick up six of them and bring them back. I also had to collect some sacred water and place it in a spring at Glastonbury Tor.

Now I'd never contemplated going on an Earth walk, or thought that I'd ever go to any of these countries I was now supposed to. I never really had any desire to. I suppose when you're young there's always that fantasy in your mind: 'Oh, I'll go to America and play Kooris and Indians.' But you usually get over that by the time you turn thirty, and I was a lot older than that.

This is how it happened. I'm sitting in the desert in the dirt with the Memees but my thoughts are about being promoted to CPO at my work. I'm thinking, 'I wonder if I'll get that manager's package done by Christmas? Gee, I'd like to be the first up to get my manager's package in. Wouldn't that be a coup! I've had all these traditional spiritual teachings, but I don't know if they've done me one bloody bit of good.'

Then I hear this voice say, 'Min will go on her Earth walk.'

And I go, 'I don't think so! I'm a CPO. I can't just go on an Earth walk.' Honestly, it's a battle with myself all the time.

It was this very old Memee speaking who then sat and drew in the sand. 'You go to this place,' she said, and drew what looked like a little altar made out of stone. It was a very good sketch. 'You pick up this stone, shaped like this.' It looked like a very tiny foetus. 'And it's this colour. This is where you pick it up — on top of the hill.' She drew again in the sand. 'There'll be grey stones and these little blue flowers and little plants with leaves curled over. This plant grows here. This plant grows there. Take this many steps from here, dig down this deep, pick up the stone — this shape, this colour, this size. This is where you go. You go to where the white people come from.'

And I thought, 'Yeah, right, somewhere on the entire planet. Is this faith or what?' Then I'm thinking, 'How am I going to get the money to pay for chasing all around the bloody world? We're talking big bucks here and I'm Miss Impoverished!'

Suddenly I thought of Stonehenge and decided this was the place she was talking about. I'm smug. I look over at the others with this knowing smile. Then I'm thinking, 'This means that I've just got to go to Stonehenge so I'll see my son on the way there. I'll book in advance and get a cheap ticket. Piece of cake!' Now I was right off in my mind, skilfully getting it all together so that I could get it done.

Get out and get back. Ego had taken me off. Then I asked, 'Who put this stone there?'

This Memee, who could barely speak English and was as old as old, answered, 'I did.'

'I don't remember her ever leaving Australia,' I thought. So I asked, 'When?'

She looked at me and, in a very croaky voice, replied, 'Five thousand years ago.'

'That's all I need to hear!' I thought. 'I'm off chasing around for a bloody myth. I'm chasing around for a fantasy.'

It challenged me because we've been taught all our lives that if you can't pick it up, look at it, feel it, it just doesn't exist. Even though I knew a lot of hard-to-believe things existed, when she said that, it was still a bit far-fetched for me. You try paying $2000 for a ticket to England to look for a stone that was put there by a woman 5000 years ago who right this minute is sitting in front of you! It tested every bit of me. That's how the Western world influences us; we come from our heads — not our Miwis.

I thought, 'I'm going to have to pay all that money to go over there. Why me, why me?' I started blaming my great granny and was tempted to take the easy way out. 'Bloody hell,' I thought, 'why don't I just go home and paint a stone and bring it back.'

The old Memee knew because she eyeballed me saying, 'I know this stone. I know every mark on it.'

So I decided against painting one to give to her because that would mean I would die big time and I'm a coward and I didn't want to die yet. I thought what was happening in my life was bizarre but still faith came back.

I was given more directions in the sand for the other stones I was to gather. The Memee told me, 'Then you go to a place where these trees grow and these flowers grow and there are lots of ponds and lakes and a river of ice and you go in there and you pick up this stone here at this lake. You'll see! It's shaped like this.'

I didn't ask who put it there; I just drew it on paper. And then I was told to go to another country where it was high and the terrain looked like Australia, to a place where the Indians were having a big corroboree. I had to sit there and wait for an Indian to come up to me.

And so it was that I was given the instructions for the stones I was to gather and those I needed to put out. And, before I knew it, I was off on an Earth walk to collect these lore/law stones that held great power and that had been placed on the Dreaming tracks over many different lifetimes.

An Earth Walk

First up, I went by plane to England. But by the time I got there I had again changed my mind. 'This is ridiculous,' I thought. 'When I get home I will look along the river for stones that look just the same.' I'd convinced myself that not only had the Memees lost the plot but so had I.

My son met my plane and I had to go straight to intensive care with heart failure. I was very sick; my heart almost gave out. Have you ever been in one of Britain's hospitals? I was in the ward with men — old fogies. I got a real fright and I just wanted to get out. I told myself, 'OK, I'll do it, I'll do it. Stonehenge, here I come.'

When I got to Stonehenge I was in for a big shock. The altar in the picture the Memee had drawn wasn't there. There was nothing that vaguely looked like it. I was beside myself, crying, 'Oooohh! I've failed. I'll go back and be totally humiliated. I hadn't really listened to what the old Memee had said because once I had decided on Stonehenge I hadn't paid proper attention to anything else she told me.

My son tried pretending that none of this was happening, so for a bit of peace he suggested we go to Ireland for a week before I went to the United States. So off we went and we're travelling around and I'm worried. I've failed on the first stone. I felt like drinking or committing suicide. I didn't do either, but I was worried.

We travelled all over Ireland and were about to head into Northern Ireland when in Galloway the first sign came. We were staying in a little village and, just as I was walking past a shop thinking, 'Oh please spirit, help me!' I looked in the window and there was this little stone Miwi. I couldn't believe my eyes. I went running into the shop and asked, 'Oh, where did you get that Miwi?' A woman replied, 'That's a little god called Ungh.' And I thought, 'It's a sign!'

I then went back to the hotel to have a sleep, because I was still really unwell. Suddenly my daughter-in-law came bursting into my room with this little postcard in her hand. 'I've found it. I've found it!' There, on the postcard, was the stone altar on the mountain. The place was called the Burran.

When we got to the Burran there were lots of English people around, and they tend to be very proper. The English and Kooris are different like that. I've got to feel and see with my Miwi. So I'm going in one direction then another — a wild woman from Australia with my hair all over the place. My son's wife is saying, 'Oh my god, can't I go back to our hotel? Look what she's doing. People will think she's insane.'

But when I'm on the scent of something I don't really care. Besides, there was too much at stake for me — like my life.

On this knoll I found the flowers and the curled leaves then took the six steps, and began to dig beside the altar. Of course no-one around said anything but, as they circled me like emus, I could read their colours. I asked myself, 'Do I say, "Excuse me, but I've come to dig up a stone that my people put here 5000 years ago?"' They wouldn't have believed me anyway. So, regardless, I dug down about 20 centimetres. I got a tiny little cut on my hand and it bled but I think it needed to bleed. The stone lay buried much deeper than I had thought. So much soil had built up in 5000 years, even underneath the altar. Then my hand started to bleed badly and I was just about to give up when I hit something. And there was this stone! Exactly the way the old Memee had described it — a tiny, jet-black foetus.

What a relief it was. I took this stone and replaced it with another one[39], just as I'd been told to do. I cleaned it and had a really good look. There were fine markings almost like carvings on it. I knew the Memee would recognise it.

The whole top of the knoll was pale grey, almost white shale. Before I left, using a piece of this shale, I carved a Miwi onto another piece of shale, making sure there were no breaks in its chalk-like outline. I put it on a jagged piece of rock that was sticking out of the ground and then broke it with another stone, which I dropped as I turned and walked away without looking back.

•••••

Then it was off to other parts of the world. It was quite easy until I got to the States where I had to chase around and find out where all the Indians were having their big corroboree. I discovered it was Santa Fe in New Mexico. But I hadn't been told how big the corroboree was going to be — and it was huge.

Remember what the Memee had told me: 'You go to this place and you sit there under this tree, and wait, and an Indian man will come.' You know, we were talking about a place many thousands of miles away and I would have to sit there for who knew how long. I could starve in the meantime. And what about the toilet? You know, the important things! 'Where's the nearest toilet to this tree?' I now wanted to ask.

So my mind was filled with all of these things. But I found a tree, I went there, and I sat. It dawned on me that in some aspects it all read like a dark comedy. The corroboree was an annual festival that lasted three weeks with people from just about every tribe of Indians on the planet. And I had to wait for an Indian!

I had a friend who met me there, she wasn't Koori, and one day she said, 'Come on down and see this.'

'I have to wait,' I said.

'You don't believe that bloody stuff,' she said. 'Come with me. Leave him a note in case he turns up.'

I ignored her and vowed I would never again take a non-Koori woman on a vision quest. So I continued sitting in this park in Sante Fe, under the tree until my butt was aching and then went completely numb. Believe me, it's hard sitting on the ground under a tree for thirteen or fourteen hours at a very high altitude when you're not used to it! So I'm thinking, 'Oh why don't I grow roots out of somewhere and become a tree and grow leaves and frigging ...' And I moaned, I always moan. I'm just one of those moaners. 'Bloody sitting here waiting for a bloody Indian who's probably been dead for fifty bloody years.' You know how you create all these things!

Then on the third day I'm still sitting there. It was about three o'clock. I'd gone through books, watched people and read their colours until I was bored to death. So I had my head down, absorbed in something extremely spiritual — like the local newspaper — and thinking, 'I just want to die. I just want to die and be free of this bullshit.' And then a shadow crossed my newspaper, and this very low voice slowly said, 'Have you been waiting long?'

I looked up and saw these big silver plaits hanging down. The face looked like sandstone along the beach, where the water's run down and cut crevices, like this old Indian was moulded from the Earth itself. His eyes were amazing. He said something like, 'I'm sorry.'

'It doesn't matter one bit,' I said quietly like a saint. But my mind was going, 'I'll be stuffed. I'll be stuffed.' I'm not very spiritual or sacred at times! Sometimes I can't believe that the teachings were given to me. This old Indian then gave me a stone and said to me, 'We've been waiting for your people in Australia to begin the new time, and we've been waiting on you. Now that you have this stone you have started it. We're waiting on the white buffalo to be born that will open the new red road.'[40]

I couldn't believe it. I could have just kissed his face clean off. He had handed me what was called the Dreamwalker stone. Then he said, 'Tomorrow you go to this place and if you wait there's an Indian spirit that will come ... He will give you three stones. Celestial stones. And you will deliver these for me.'

I won't even tell you what I was thinking. I could feel my shoulders sag. 'Now I'm doing everybody's bidding!' I thought. 'What happens if he sends me to Alaska?' Not very gracious of me but I did mellow out later and had to apologise profusely. At the time I didn't quite know what to say, but then he said to me, 'You go to this spot and you stand and you wait and the stones will just manifest.'

My life is about faith, it really is about faith. I needed to call on all my resources to get myself going. When you're consistently bombarded with such a spiritually shallow world it is hard to keep this faith in balance. If you've ever been in Sante Fe in the summer, you'll know it's hot. It's like the devil lives next door. So I went early in the morning because he said to go at a certain time and wait. It was nice, dewy, with a little breeze, really nice. And I waited and waited and waited. Then I started to cook and then I started to say the 'f' word a lot. Because I had no hat and I was thirsty, I had no water — I had nothing. I'm thinking, 'I don't believe this. You're an intelligent woman. You've got a mind. You're standing here, your brains are half-fried and you're waiting for stones to manifest from the Earth, stones that come from a celestial being. And what about the manager's package?'

So I was without shade, it was very hot and I was there for hours. I kept turning round and round, willing the stones to appear as I thought, 'Why didn't they send someone else? It's easy to see there's a conspiracy against me.'

I got into that 'poor me' pity mode. 'What did I do in the last twelve months that's upset all the old teachers? Have I always upset them?' I wondered. 'I don't know how much longer I can stand here without absolutely dropping dead from this heat.'

I don't know how long it was, but I just kept on thinking 'poor me'. I remember going through all this stuff and then coming out the other side telling myself, 'Well fuck it, I'm here now and there's no way in the world I'm going to move from here and miss this.'

So I sighed, closed my eyes and let it all go. I grounded myself. When I opened my eyes I saw above the mesa an Indian holding a golden yellow skin. It was so soft and fine. When I first saw the skin I thought it was in the shape of a shield and four symbols were within a circle burnt into it. One symbol resembled the sun. Then three stones were right in front of me on the ground. They looked like moonstones but I can't say I picked them up graciously. In fact I grabbed them in fear of them disappearing again.

•••••

After all that I then travelled up to Canada to pick up the last stone I needed to gather. The whole walk took me about eight weeks but eventually I had gone all the way around, and I came back home to Australia. I had been asked to gather six stones and I brought all six back with me. I hadn't thought one bit about being asked about them at Customs but I got them through.

I also came home with the three celestial stones. They reminded me of moonstones. Each one of them has its meaning — the Journey Stone, the Moon Energy Stone and the Rebirth Stone. If you hold these stones in your hand, you receive Dreaming track energy.

The Dreamwalker stone is just a little black stone. It is a prophecy stone. And they said to me, 'Look into the stone. What do you see?' And I thought, 'What am I supposed to see?' No one had told me anything. So I sat with the stone and turned it over. And then many images appeared — bears, kangaroos, and wombats. I got up to 134 different animals out of that one little stone. I didn't want to part with it. It was like, 'Good, yeah, wow!' It was divine to hold. It was really a treasure. I wondered if I could hide this stone and go to a shop and then produce the one I'd purchased. But anyway I couldn't — and I didn't. It had been a test of greed.

I thought that the Dreamwalker stone came from North America because the old Indian had called it their Dreamwalker stone. But months later, after I came home from my Earth walk, a friend showed me a gem book that had fallen at her feet in a bookstore, opened at a page with stones that looked like the Dreamwalker stone. On the page it said that the stones were fragments of meteorites and only found in certain parts of Western Australia and the Northern Territory. So now the stone had come home. I had done what I'd been called upon to do — I had brought back my share of the stones.

•••••

There were also stones that I needed to put in place. One stone I was unable to place was for a break in the Dreaming tracks in the Andes, Peru. The place where the light needed to be joined is on a mountain. It's up high, and there are buildings made of stone. Once the people there were very, very holy. They were invaded and absolutely massacred, their city was destroyed and so they left, their city abandoned. However, there's a tree growing there. It's not unlike the Australian native frangipani plant, but it's a big tree. And beneath that tree is a temple that remains untouched.

On my return home to Australia I discovered that because of the high altitude in Sante Fe the lower lobe of my left lung had collapsed.

It was too late to re-inflate it and I was warned not to go to high altitudes again. Several years later I found a young lad to take the stone that I had been given to this place and he buried it under the tree for me.

Throughout this whole trip it was amazing how people were put in my path. It was strange for me to see Indigenous people who were so fair. I'd always imagined all Indigenous people to be coffee-coloured, chocolate-coloured or just outright black.

And I learnt so much else too. When I was in England I was told that the Celts had planted a New Age cross at Glastonbury Tor on 29 April 1990. I also found out that the sacred stone of New Zealand had gone around the world. Then I learnt that the Indigenous people of Greenland had their own stones. Many years later I met an Australian woman of Celtic origin who was returning sacred stones to where they belonged along the Dreaming tracks. This was to help with the alignment of the planet onto its new path and to bring the balance about more quickly. It seems many peoples from many nations had been gathering, moving or replacing sacred stones, sometimes without knowing why.

All along, this movement of stones was re-aligning the Dreaming tracks and increasing the rate at which our Miwis were awakening. Then things began to really happen. It didn't matter how much money we had or how satisfying our careers were, without our Miwis being awake and on their journeys these things were no good to us. That's why at this time so many people just walked away from their careers to live somewhere in the bush. They were either on a spirit walk or an Earth walk — seeking their spiritual responsibility.

The stirring of awareness, the awakening of our Miwis, is still happening. And colour has nothing to do with it. It's happening in England, it's happening in Canada, it's happening in the United States where the Native Americans are now rapidly strengthening their spirituality because they, like my people, have a relatively short history of Miwi contamination and suppression from the introduction of religion and their dispossession from the Oneness.

Moving to the New Dreaming Track

It took six years for the Dreaming tracks of our planet to slowly open to energise the regeneration of the Earth. No-one could escape Biami's lore/law. All this means that no matter what colour or creed they are, everybody, every adult over thirty, has to take responsibility for their actions. Now, neither power nor money could any longer save you or help hide what you were doing. From 1990 until the present day there have been more leaders, politicians and powerful, rich, wealthy people prosecuted than ever before in the history of this country. And it's been happening overseas too.

The old people knew a whole range of things would happen because breaking Biami's stones meant that the Earth was changing its course. Some said the weather would change and the sea would change. Such things will occur, even if gradually. But eventually the sea will be in the middle of the desert again and there will be renewed land once more.

The change of course might be a very tiny change, but it is having catastrophic affects. As the Dreaming tracks have opened and remained open during the last sixteen years everything has been shaken up and moved rapidly so there have been changes in the Earth. During this period most of the bad earthquakes, volcanic eruptions, tidal waves and weird weather have occurred. People have tried to explain such things by talking about global warming and melting icecaps or the end of the world and so on. But this is not all that has been going on. Much more than this has been happening.

Think of it this way. We're all used to walking at a certain pace, we are comfortable with this but if we are forced to walk at a pace like a marathon walker it can throw us. We can become anxious, stressed and behave differently perhaps without realising it.

Our planet is a living female — a fertile, living female. And because she's been spinning at a certain speed for a long time, as her speed changes parts of her body shift about and things get upset. So volcanic eruptions, earthquakes and tidal waves occur.

•••••

We're moving onto a Dreaming track of a higher spiritual awareness. But before we can be there, we must deal with our garbage. This means the releasing of much negative energy which otherwise can build up to wars and chaos. It's like being on a beach with what looks like pure beautiful sand and you collect some of this sand and put it in a box. Then you take the box and shake it up and you are amazed at the impurities and rubbish that have come to the surface. And this is what the old people say is happening right now. Chaos is happening because of all that is coming to the surface. But now we can see how impure everything is and how much unrevealed rubbish we're still carrying around.

In order to deal with this rubbish you've got to see it and know it's there. It's like going to a linen press after a decade of it not being opened, and giving it a good clean out and thinking, 'Was that really there for that long?' When you live in a house things build up and it's full of spiders and cobwebs because the build-up's been ignored. Negativity has got to be dealt with; it's got to be cleaned all the time — working and cleansing all the time, from within.

Some of the teachings say the destruction of the Earth will be by fire, with volcanic eruptions. But I believe it can happen as a massive black hole. Our negativity can take us there, into a big black hole, spiritually and psychologically, creating endless dark nights of the soul.

Also remember that the planet passes through a Dreaming track that has leftovers from the War of the Dreaming. During our passage this time we're moving through an era of big meteorite remnants and there is a danger of different spots on the planet being hit by these.

The likelihood of war has become greater as the changing spin of the Earth leaves us feeling jittery and anxious and then we are easily provoked into fear. And remember, often fear is wearing anger's clothing. People may feel that they are surrounded by threats, which they sense are everywhere — from their partners, families, communities, both inside and outside their countries. Politicians exploit this condition. Everyone should be staying calm, grounded — as individuals, in our relationships, in our homes and at work. Otherwise with all the shifting and shaking that is happening disagreements and divisions can flare up quickly.

Essentially things can become nasty. People can do bad things. It's inevitable; these things will happen and need to happen. Many people could think, 'I've just got to give up because this is too great, too powerful. I can't face it.' But we can't run, because we are the only ones who can fix it now. In a lot of teachings I've heard you only need a pinhead of faith. We've just got to stay grounded in our faith. It's important that people don't panic — and that people don't give up. We have to come back and think about the innocent and be prepared to make a stand.

Many people will abandon each other, and abandon their animals too. But we need to take care of the animals. And we need to take care of each other. One thing I know for sure is this: that if somebody threatened or tried to hurt my children or my grandchildren in front of me, I would protect them. That's a fact. They would have to come and harm me first! I know for certain I would do everything to protect my children and grandchildren, because that's who I am.

But still I think we will make it. When the stones were broken everything started coming to the surface so we can now see all the 'shit' in and around us. The more the light shines on us, the more truth is revealed. We can be disillusioned and ashamed because we see exactly who we are, warts and all. But this can also give us the energy and strength to accept and forgive ourselves, starting with those around us, and to extend out from there onto the path of forgiving everybody. That way we can develop and validate the essence of Biami we have within us. It's going to be as easy as giving up chocolate!

As many people's Miwis awaken, and as they take this awareness into their minds, they just change. For instance, people with enormous wealth may give half of it away to schemes to tree the deserts. It is almost like a tussle between the realms of heaven and hell.

Closing the Dreaming Tracks

It was said that the Dreaming tracks, having been opened in May 1990, would take six years to become fully open. They would stay open for ten years from May 1996, and at 7.30 pm on 7 May 2006 the stones would have to be re-carved and put back where they belong. This would start the closing of the tracks, which would take another six years, and they would be fully closed by 2012. So the full cycle would take twenty-two years.

As 2006 approached, many of us realised that we didn't have much time to prepare before the stones had to be re-carved. If we hadn't got ourselves together and if we hadn't woken up enough by this date then we'd be in trouble. At that time we were going through some of the hardest times we'd ever gone through in this planet's history.

The re-carving of the stones in 2006 was to be done by the people who broke them in 1990. I was told to re-carve a stone, dressed just as I was when I broke the stone in Redfern, and then go to my next destination. The lore/law stones are detailed. When carving them the designs must be executed exactly, otherwise there can be disastrous consequences to the planet — and whoever is doing the carving. A number of those who had broken the stones had died in the meantime, so their areas became Dreaming pockets or places of light. A descendant along the deceased person's lineage will, at some time, re-carve the stones instead.

The final lore/law stones, although carved by Biami and given to us as a last resort to bring us back to our connection of Oneness and save ourselves from destruction, have nowhere near the same power to create the Dreaming pockets as Biami. They are not the same as the pockets of the Creation left untouched by the War of the Dreaming when Biami instructed Wahwee to bring the great floods. Dreaming pockets are only a fraction as powerful as these original pockets of the Dreaming.

Remember, a Dreaming pocket is a power pocket where you are more open to knowledge coming in through guides and you are more aware of both how significant and insignificant we are in the Oneness. Dreaming pockets will draw certain kinds of people — keepers of the earth who ensure the continuity of everything and those who strive to walk their talk. Dreaming pockets also disrobe our denial and magnify our ability to break through delusion and our sense of powerlessness. We are then no longer victims and it becomes easier to take responsibility.

It can be difficult to explain some of these things. I can only go on how I have interpreted what I have been taught. You've got to remember that I get the teachings from people who often don't speak much English. There's usually an interpreter who speaks five or six dialects. And the knowledge is passed on like that, although some of the old women do know English.

All this means that the Earth will now regenerate herself. She'll shake us up in the meantime however, and the old people indicate there will be a lot of sacrifice. What part does humankind play in all of this? From our traditional perspective, as in a lot of other teachings, man does not have dominion over everything. What man has done over the centuries is set himself above everything else as a supreme power. And that's not how it is, because everything living is part human — that's the lore/law. So, if a man separates himself from everything he becomes a grain of sand. And a grain of sand in a strong wind will blow away. If man accepts that he's only a very small part of something bigger, like the trees, like the Earth, like the animals, and everything on this planet and in countless universes, and if he truly becomes part of all this then, from a spiritual level, this grain of sand will be embedded into the most solid mountain, one that no wind can shift. This is what the teachings say.

The New Dreaming Track

The teachings are about a higher consciousness of the Oneness. Your awareness is so heightened that, for example, you find yourself suddenly questioning how living cattle are stored for slaughter. You'll be aware of how people treat each other — it could be how you're being treated or how you are treating others. You're awakening to the truth as it is being revealed.

The teachings of this new Dreaming track can be taught in many ways — orally, by 'thoughting', or through visions and meditation. Whether we call it Miwi, spirit or heart/mind, our knowing is awakened. If we choose not to live by this knowing then we might as well not have had it in the first place.

When the stones were broken and the Dreaming Tracks re-opened, the feminine lore/law was brought back, given back. Up it came, and as we were moving onto a new Dreaming track women began to get the power. Because the power comes through Nungeena-tya, Biami gave the healing of the planet to the feminine. The men had had their turn as leaders.

So what are we women to do? We can point the finger of blame: 'Look at the world we've inherited. We didn't start all this.' And it's true, we didn't. So we could just close our minds and not think about it or take responsibility for the part we have played in it. Every son who started a war had a mother. I've lived long enough now to know many, many women who had daughters yet as soon as they had a son their daughters became as insignificant as their unwanted pets and their son become their god.

As I have explained earlier, a circle of women decided to teach the women's teachings to everyone partly because there were elements in the breaking of the stones that all women have to learn. All women have to be shown the way back to honouring Nungeena-tya, themselves and each other. Women have lost their honour in many ways. You see it every day. They see another woman's husband — they want him, they take him. They see a child's father — they want him, they take him. Then their shame catches up with them so they blame the man.

There would not be one broken marriage and there would be no infidelity if every woman said, 'Go home to your woman! I won't do this. Go home to your babies! Just go home!' So I'm not saying we women are bad but rather that we can say and do bad things. And I am saying we must cut away the delusion, for God's sake, and look at who we really are. We're not perfect. In fact, we women are bloody imperfect, so we're greedy!

It is not up to us to teach the men; it is up to the men to teach the men. That's what is meant by men's business. It is up to the women to teach women about honouring themselves, each other and Nungeena-tya. When we achieve this — and we can — there will be no more stolen husbands and fathers and we can concentrate on regenerating the Earth. This is women's business; this is women's lore/law. There are no excuses. We have to honour ourselves as women, honour our mothers and honour mothering. There is no more honour left for mothering and so there is no honour for Nungeena-tya, our mother who provides all that we need all of our lives. So, as a result, she is dying and all that a lot of us are doing is nothing but standing on the sidelines saying, 'Why doesn't somebody do something?'

As I see it there are four kinds of people in the world. Well, three kinds really — the fourth is sort of sleeping. There are those who ask 'What should happen?', those who watch what happens, and those who look around in a daze and ask 'What happened?' The fourth kind is those who can make things happen — and this can be us.

But listen to me, if you take this on you could cop a kicking from people, perhaps even abuse from your family and friends. You could be disowned because you might say things like 'Just because they're Arab doesn't make them dangerous' or 'Just because they're Pakistani or Afghan doesn't make them a terrorist'. But don't give up — not after all the hard work that you and other women have done. It will be so easy to give up, but don't.

Only we as women can change the way we think about our mother, the planet. Only we can change the way we behave to each other and only we can teach our children a different way.

What We Can Do to Stabilise

Now is the time of love and feminine sacrifice because when the stones were broken the universal energy was given to Nungeena-tya, the all-powerful Mother. And because all that is feminine grows from her, this is the time of the feminine.

Love means sacrifice. Love means you care enough. You don't have to love your neighbour; you don't have to love your brother. You just have to have a love for the essence of Biami that's in every person.

Because the stones were broken, power was given back to our Spirit, and that's why I believe that we'll make it. If everyone decided that they would take responsibility just for themselves, and not worry about anybody else, and if everyone took responsibility for the environment around them and became part of something bigger, rather than being autonomous and setting themselves apart from everything else, then I think we could make it. It's a hard road, and as I've said there's going to be a lot of upheaval and disturbance along the way. But if we are able to come back to a balance and look at need rather than greed, if we accept ourselves for who we really are, warts and all, then we'll start to accept other people. All around the world right now there's an awakening of Spirit. Every day we need to get up and ask, 'Today, will I meet my needs or will I meet my greed?' Everyday that's what we should do.

And we need to teach our children. Years ago the first gardening you taught your children was planting radish seeds because they grew so fast. How many times now do we take our children out and connect them to the Earth? Watch someone who's garden mad, they're so grounded, they're in the Earth all the time. They're grounded because all their negative energy is absorbed, that's what Nungeena-tya's for. You must have your shoes off for at least ten minutes a day and stand barefooted on the Earth. When your kids get really angry don't say, 'Go to your room.' Instead say, 'Go straight to the yard! And gimme your shoes!' Watch what happens in ten minutes! Without fail, every single time, whenever you're angry take your shoes off and go and stand out on the Earth. Come after me if this doesn't work! Within ten minutes you are absolutely back down and grounded. We must do this every day otherwise we're just not grounded.

As I have mentioned, the changing vibration of Nungeena-tya can make us feel jittery. Swinging on a swing or in a hammock for ten minutes can allow our vibrational balance to be restored. Being around — or floating in — naturally moving water can do the same thing.

Always remember, everything starts with you. We're born boss of self, we walk our journey boss of self, and we die boss of self. It's true. Take me, for example. Just in the last few years I've ballooned. I've got all cushiony. And I mightn't like that because I'm so vain. I am! So I could allow the media hype to make me feel worthless, ugly and as unwanted as an old overstuffed armchair. Or I could tell myself that it's the oldest wood that makes the hottest fire! I'm aware that I am vain because that's what I am.

You have to look at who you are. You have to be contented with who you are. You really have to go into yourself and say, 'This is me! Yes, I'm this age or that age, and I'm happy with me.' You can't accept anyone else for who they are until you accept you for who you are. And this can be a really big challenge.

•••••

Please don't feel the situation for humanity is hopeless and futile. It is not. The stones were broken because, yes, we do have it in us to make a difference. We can change. We can hold a lemon and we can start with its story — the tree it came from, the size of the tree, the mother of that tree, how that tree came to Creation and the very first lemon seed. That's some of its story.

We need to know our own story — where we came from, our mother, our father, our country, our teachings, our strengths and weaknesses. This is the beginning of the essence of our story because it's the essence we are trying to understand. We then have the opportunity to feel someone else's spirit by walking in their shoes and starting to know their essence, their story.

But I can tell you that we are in trouble. We are still facing our destruction of Nungeena-tya and it is said that we will finally destroy ourselves. We can no longer afford to ignore the fact that we have to do something. There will continue to be one thing after another to deal with, and each of us can only come forward and say, 'This is my opportunity to make a difference.' The only power, the only real help we are going to get lies within ourselves.

There needs to be people who make the changes happen. Now, most of us have family and children and partners. But remember, none of us can take responsibility for anybody else. As desperately as we might want to, we can't interfere with another's path. We must only change ourselves. What I mean here is 'walking your talk'. That's what it's about. You might have an opinion on how this should happen or how that should happen. But you can really only change you. Participate fully in life, and as you walk along your path of doing, others will see what you are doing and join you. That's the way things will change. This is why the teachings are so very important.

The lore/law really is back. The breaking of the stones brought the Miwi awakening of all those people on the planet suffering from spiritual lostness and spiritual malnutrition. Words had failed to awaken our Miwis. But with the breaking of the stones creating an energy input from Biami into Nungeena-tya, the lore/law keepers now realised that the teachings had been kept to only a select few because so many had forgotten the original lore/law, been uninformed, or had lost the lore/law through the spiritual dislocation caused by colonisation and genocide. Also, many had said that non-Aboriginal people, because they were bad and evil, could not have these teachings. This way of thinking came from a fearful, ignorant, punishing and unforgiving place. As I have said, my understanding of the lore/law is that if you are born of this land you are of this land. So anyone, Aboriginal or not, who disobeys the teachings and contravenes the traditional lore/law is breaking the lore/law of this land. She will be walking a journey of lies, confusion and anger — a path of spiritual lostness. Everyone needs an opportunity to understand and learn the lore/law.

As I have said earlier in this book, we cannot attain a higher spiritual consciousness on our new Dreaming track and continue to destroy our teaching place, our mother Nungeena-tya. We are, under the lore/law, the keepers of this Creation of Biami.

Remember, in the Rivers of the Dreaming there are many islands but there is only one teaching place. This is where we come to learn two things: all truth and all knowledge. The teaching place is here, on mother Earth. And if our planet is destroyed there will be no possible path for us and we will not be able to elevate to any other islands in the Dreaming.

ENDNOTES

[1] For further explanation of the breaking of Biami's stones refer to Chapter 10.

[2] Uri wasn't born there; Biami sent her to the sun later.

[3] Sometimes plants spontaneously grew where Biami did healings. One of these is the turpentine tree. The sap, which should never be gathered by destroying the tree if it is to be effective, is one of the most powerful natural antiseptics. To extract the sap of the turpentine, cut a 'V' hole into the bark of the tree and attach a cup. The tree will ooze a bright yellowy, orange sap. Boil this. Add it to the bathwater for a newborn baby and also add to the water used to wash the baby's clothes. A solution should be used to wash sick people in hospital who have had surgery. It will prevent golden staph infections. It came from the Rivers of the Dreaming through Biami, so it is more powerful than anything that is only Earth manifested.

[4] Some further explanation about Dreaming tracks is that they were the paths of the Creator beings (super beings) who created images from their own essence. The tracks are the paths they walked. The Creator beings were not of this Earth so their tracks are pure light. The Creator beings went back to the Rivers of the Dreaming.

[5] A further explanation about negative Dreaming tracks is that the giant green ants etc are not Creator beings and when these bugeenge beings die and are buried on the Dreaming tracks it creates that which then becomes negative.

[6] For further explanation of 'the awakening of the Miwi and bringing back the lore/law' refer to Chapter 10.

[7] The dahwee is the sheath enveloping the Miwi. See Chapter 5 for further explanation.

[8] See the 'Teaching Story on Compassion' in Chapter 8.

[9] See the 'Teaching Story on Acceptance and Unconditional Love' in Chapter 8.

[10] This refers to my seeing of people's auras.

[11] Refer also to Chapter 6.

[12] For a song to be sung refer to 'How to Conduct a Birthing Ceremony' in Chapter 6.

[13] Refer to 'Born on the Songlines' in Chapter 4.

[14] For further information refer to 'Songlines for Nienjoh: Honey Grevillea' in Chapter 4.

[15] Refer to 'The Story of Burradahn, Son of Biami' in Chapter 3.

[16] Refer to Chapter 2.

[17] Refer to 'Songlines for Nienjoh: She-oak' in Chapter 4.

[18] Refer to 'Rebirthing Ceremony' in Chapter 5.

[19] Refer to 'Boori' section in this chapter for more information.

[20] Refer to 'How to Conduct a Birthing Ceremony' in Chapter 6.

[21] Refer to 'The Miwi Print' in Chapter 5.

[22] Refer to 'How to Conduct a Birthing Ceremony' in Chapter 6.

[23] Refer to 'Boodthong' section in Chapter 7.

[24] Refer to Chapter 5.

[25] Refer to 'Born on the Songlines' in Chapter 4.

[26] Refer to 'Miwi Connectedness Maintenance' in Chapter 5.

[27] Refer to Glossary.

[28] Refer to Chapter 5.

[29] Refer to Chapter 3.

[30] Refer to Chapter 3.
[31] Refer to Chapter 2.
[32] Refer to 'Dreaming Tracks' in Chapter 3.
[33] Refer to 'Dreaming Tracks' in Chapter 3.
[34] Refer to Chapter 9.
[35] After Biami's stones were broken at some time in the future one crystal would rise again from the depths of the ocean and both crystals would go back to where they belong in Biami's cave at the bottom of the sacred mountain. Then once again Biami could come back and help humanity.
[36] Refer to Chapter 9.
[37] Refer to Chapter 1.
[38] Years later a woman from New Zealand sent me a book called *The Song of the Stones*. It was about the green sacred stone of New Zealand. Their legends are quite different to ours, of course, but the old Maori people had chosen to break this stone at the same time.
[39] At some stage I need to go back to the Burran and get this stone I placed there.
[40] From what I understand, their higher enlightenment or spirit has to do with what they call 'the red road'. And in March 1996, just before the Dreaming tracks were fully opened, the white buffalo was born.

GLOSSARY

This glossary contains words I have drawn from the Wirradjirri, Gurindji and other New South Wales Aboriginal languages. Some words are from one language, some from another and some are blended. Traditionally there was no 's' in the Wirradjirri language.

Arrernte: Indigenous nation in Central Australia

Bahloo: the Moon

bahrook: first human

ballahng: silly woman

Biami: Creator, God

billinga: magpie

birik: a spirit in human form, a ghost

boodthoong: infant

boorai: fart

boori: child

bora: men's ceremonial ground

bugeenge: bad; bad spirit

bunya: tree of knowledge, sacred nuts

bunyip: water monster

Burradahn: Son of Biami

buundi: a weapon like a club

colours: a person's aura

coolamon: a container, used by women to carry bush tucker, water, babies; an all-purpose carrier, gifted in marriage ceremony

dahwie: the sheath enveloping a Miwi; it has an opening above your head that allows for the channelling of universal light

doodle: penis

doonday dardeman doonday: swearing

duubai: young female wanai

Gadtjirrka: Dreaming, lore/law

gardjya: man

gidgi: a type of wood used to make ceremonial sticks

gidgin: berries

Girrah: the Wind Spirit

Goolooga: the Mother of the Stars, a sacred mountain on the south coast of New South Wales

goongi: good

Gurinji: my great grandmother's ancestry

jillawah: toilet

jindai jupun: brother and sister

jirrimah: mountain

kadaitchi/kadaicha: clever man, feather foot, teacher-healer, lore/law keeper

Kimillaroi: an Indigenous nation in northern New South Wales, including the Moree area

kuracha: the white cockatoo, a messenger

Koori: us people of the NSW and Victorian Aboriginal nations

maroodtha: big

Memee: Grandmother; old woman

migai: woman

Mimi: Spirit (*can't be trusted*)

Mirrah: Spirit of Spring; Biami's daughter

Miwi: Spirit, soul (*not to be confused with birik*)

moogeenge: blind

moogil: stupid

Mootwingee: a sacred place, north of Broken Hill

mullawahl: the protective sheath that seals the Miwi, between the Miwi and dahwie

Murri: an Aboriginal person from northern NSW and Queensland

Muulbung: a Wirradjirri lore/law man; a kadaitchi who was alive when I was a child

Nungeena-tya: Mother Earth

Nunga: South Australian Aboriginal person

nurrigah: mad (*from the word nyrahbung*)

nyrahbung: mental as anything

Ogkteringa/Okeringa: women's teaching stones

Parkingee: the Indigenous nation to the west of the Wirradjirri nation, including the area around Wilcannia, Broken Hill, Dareton and Wentworth

quandong: a desert fruit tree, found in my country, from Biami's own garden

rorah: a piece of timber tied with kangaroo sinew; a message sender, used by the men to call Biami to ceremony

the Tall Ones: seven unmanifested male spirit guides; they have always visited me

Tjuringa: men's teaching stones

Uluru: once commonly known as Ayer's Rock

Uri: the Sun

waddi buundi: a short, thick wooden club with filed back root protuberances

wadjilla: a white woman

Wahwee: water spirit

wanai: puberty (*from 12–15 to 30 years of age*)

Wandjina: a spirit ancestor

warrigul: dingo

Wirradjirri: my tribe

wirrinun: a kadaitchi gone bugeenge; a law/lore breaker

wirrloo: a powerful woman healer, a teacher of the lore/law

wirrly: tornado

wongaibon: stuffed up, back to front

Wuuluumbin: Mount Warning in northern New South Wales; the cloud and lightning gatherer

yarron: a tree associated with a teaching of 'How Death Came to Be'

yathandah: emu bush

yidarrki: didgeridoo

yinarr: woman